earrings, earrings, earrings!™

Edited by Barb Switzer

earrings, earrings, earrings!

EDITOR Barb Switzer
ART DIRECTOR Brad Snow
PUBLISHING SERVICES DIRECTOR Brenda Gallmeyer
ASSISTANT ART DIRECTOR Nick Pierce
MANAGING EDITOR Barb Sprunger
COPY SUPERVISOR Michelle Beck
COPY EDITOR Amanda Ladig
TECHNICAL EDITOR Brooke Smith
PHOTOGRAPHY SUPERVISOR Tammy Christian
PHOTOGRAPHY Matt Owen
PHOTO STYLIST Tammy Steiner
GRAPHIC ARTS SUPERVISOR Ronda Bechinski
GRAPHIC ARTIST Nicole Gage
PRODUCTION ASSISTANTS Marj Morgan, Judy Neuenschwander

Printed in the United States of America
First Printing: 2009
Library of Congress Number: 2008932157
Softcover ISBN: 978-1-59217-249-8
Hardcover ISBN: 978-1-59217-239-9

DRGbooks.com

2 3 4 5 6 7 8 9

welcome

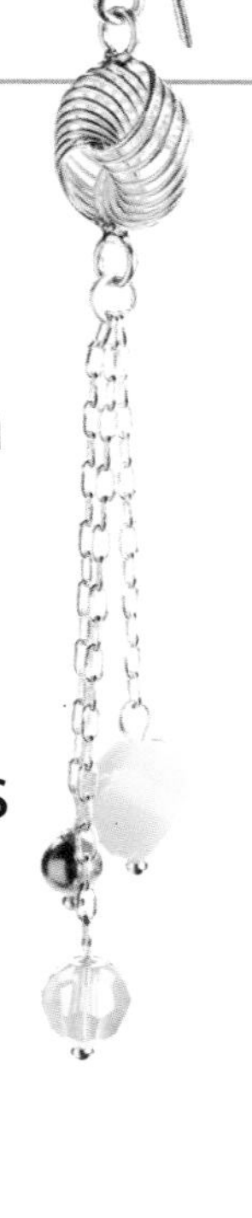

In terms of style, no jewelry form has had a longer history of popularity than earrings. Going further back than the pyramids, earrings were one of the first ways humans chose to adorn themselves. What could be better than an accessory that draws eyes to your face by framing it beautifully?

If anyone asked me what type of jewelry project is the simplest to learn, I would definitely say, "Earrings!". Earrings are a perfect way to learn the basics of jewelry making. Intermediate-level projects are included for more experienced beaders, making it simple to build skills until you can make any pair in the book. Photo step-by-step instructions take all the guesswork out of learning new techniques, and a helpful visual glossary of basic beading tools and supplies lets you see what you need.

Earrings are perfect gifts and a fast way to give a familiar outfit a whole new twist. More than 70 original designs include posts, hoops, short and long dangles, plus a few necklace and bracelet sets in case earrings are not enough to satisfy your need to bead. Add a little zing to your wardrobe with earrings, earrings and more earrings!

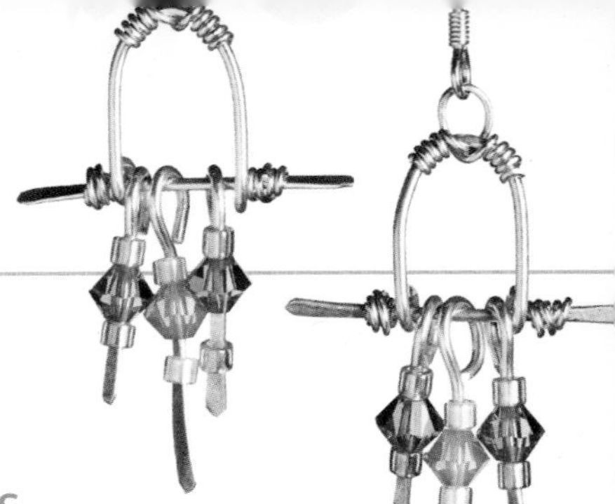

contents

hoops & posts

short dangles

long dangles

sets

visual glossary

TOOLS

Crimping pliers are for just what their name implies, crimping! The back slot puts a seam in the middle of the crimp tube, separating the ends of the flex wire and trapping it firmly. The front slot rounds out the tube and turns it into a small, tidy bead.

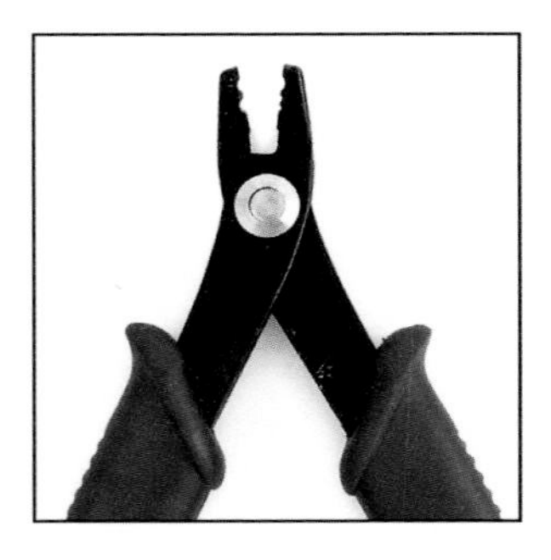

Chain-nose pliers are the most useful tool in your entire toolbox. For holding, opening and closing jump rings and bending sharp angles.

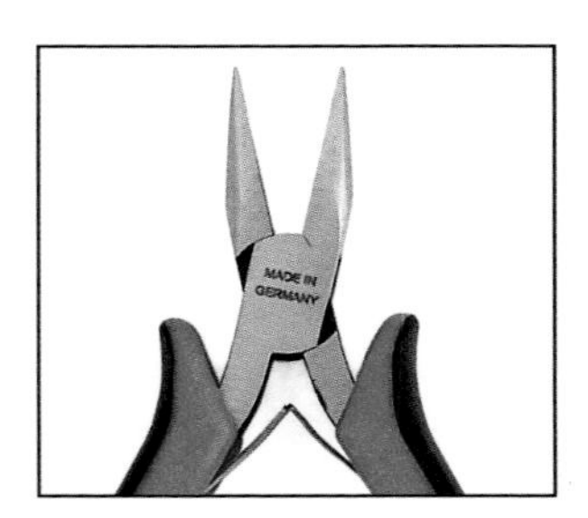

Round-nose pliers are intended for turning round loops. They do not work well for holding or grasping since they tend to leave a small dent.

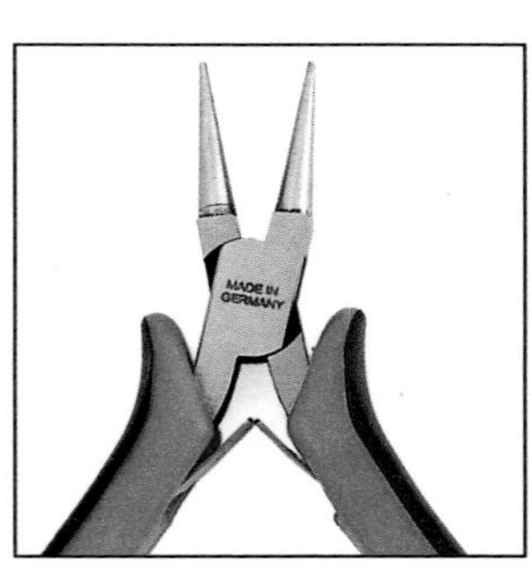

Flat-nose pliers are a wire power tool. They are excellent for turning sharp corners, holding items and for opening and closing jump rings.

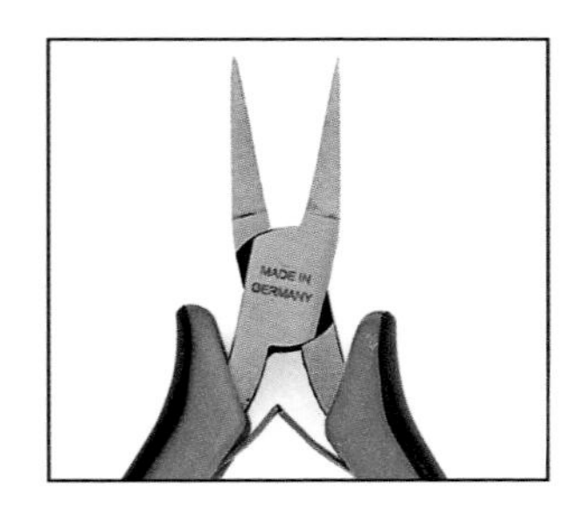

Wire flush cutters leave one flat side and one pointed side on each cut. Using flush cutters is especially important when working with heavy gauges of wire (20-gauge or smaller). One side of the cutter is flat and the other is indented.

Nylon-jaw pliers can be used to harden or straighten wire.

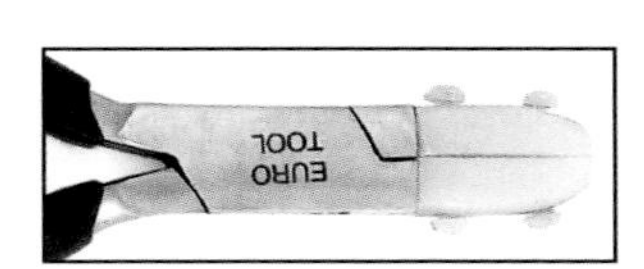

Jeweler's hammers have fine, smooth curved heads to leave a clean impression. The round peen side works well for texturing wire and metal sheet.

A bench block is a flat, smooth piece of hardened steel. Hammering on top of a block flattens out and hardens the wire. Bench blocks are also used for stamping metal to get a clean impression.

MATERIALS

Eye Pins are wires with a loop on one end and a straight portion of wire where beads can be strung. Length and gauges vary; most earrings use 24-gauge eye pins from 1½–2½ inches.

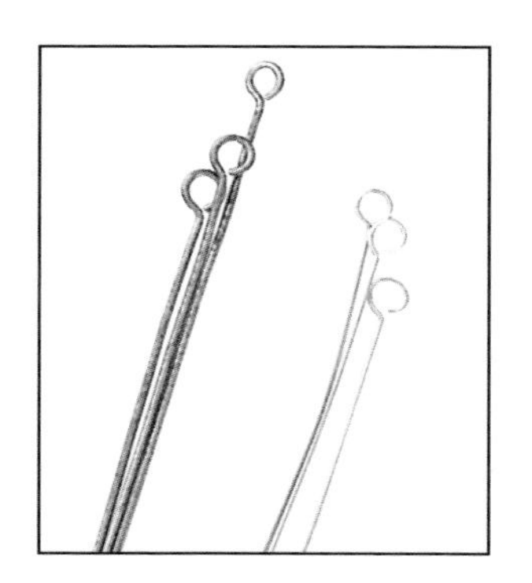

Head Pins are a piece of wire with a stop end like a fine nail head. A bead slides onto the head pin and stops on the head. Lengths and gauges vary; most earrings use 24-gauge head pins from 1½–2½ inches.

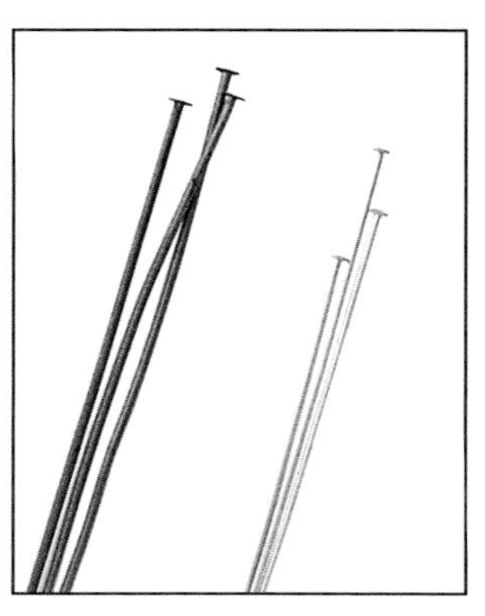

Jump Rings are one of the most versatile findings used in jewelry-making. They come in all sizes, gauges and metals. They are measured by diameter (width) and gauge (weight).

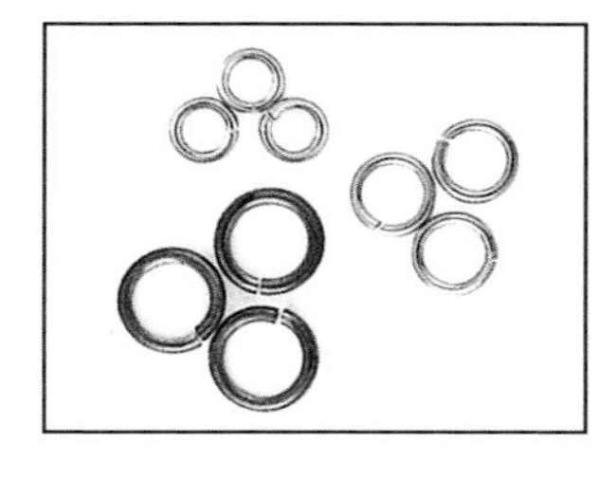

Ear Wires come in many different styles. Regular fishhook style are the most common and the easiest to make yourself. Recommended weight for ear wires is either 22- or 20-gauge.

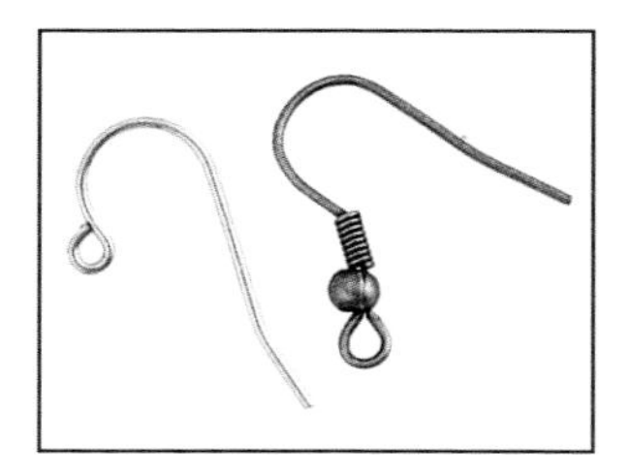

Crimp Tubes are small soft metal cylinders that can be flattened or formed around flexible beading wire to secure the ends. They are an essential component for bead stringing projects.

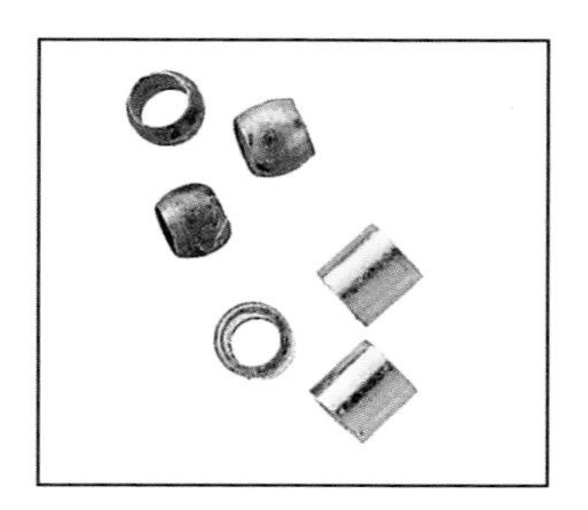

Wire comes in many sizes or *gauges*. Gauge is the measured diameter of the wire. The higher the number, the thinner the wire. Wire can be tempered soft, half-hard or hard, which refers to its stiffness. Copper, silver and gold-filled are most commonly used for jewelry.

Flexible Beading Wire comes in several weights from .010–.026-inch-diameter and is designed for stringing. It is available in precious metal and several colors and is made from 7 to 49 strands of steel wire, twisted and encased in a flexible plastic coating. Ends are finished with crimp beads using either crimping or chain-nose pliers.

basics step by step

Creating your own beaded jewelry is easy and only takes a few tools. Practice these techniques using less expensive metal findings. Once your finishing techniques are perfected, use real sterling silver or vermeil (real gold plating over sterling silver) to add elegance to your beadwork.

OPENING & CLOSING JUMP RINGS

Jump rings are one of the most versatile findings used in jewelry-making. They come in all sizes and gauges.

Use two pairs of smooth chain-nose pliers (bent or flat-nose pliers work fine as a second plier). (Photo A)

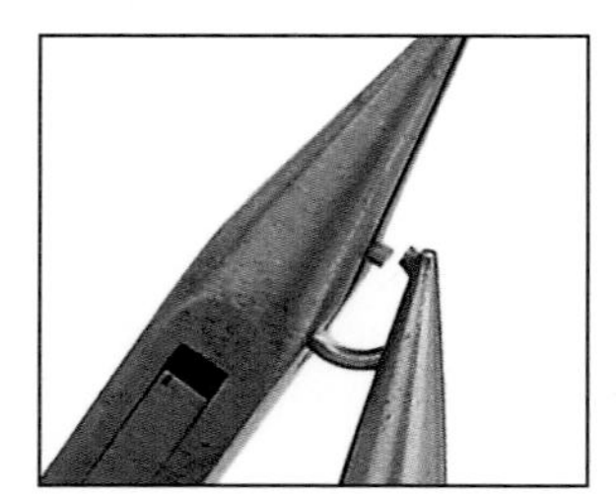

Photo A

Push ring open with right plier while holding across the ring with left plier. To close, hold in the same way and rock the ring back and forth until ring ends rub against each other or you hear a click. Moving the ring past closed then back hardens the ring and assures a tight closure. (Photo B)

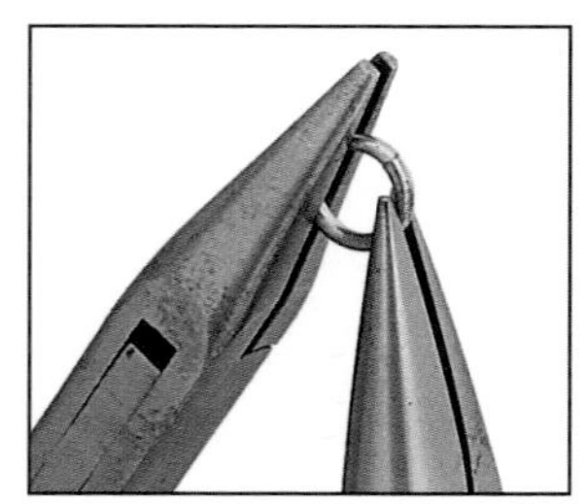

Photo B

MAKING AN EYE PIN OR ROUND LOOP

Eye pins should be made with half-hard wire to make sure they hold their shape. 22-gauge will fit through most beads, with the exception of many semi-precious stones. Most Czech glass beads and 4mm crystals will fit on 20-gauge wire.

The length used for the eye loop depends on how big you want the loop. Here we will use 3/8 inch for a moderate size loop.

Flush trim end of wire. (Photo A)

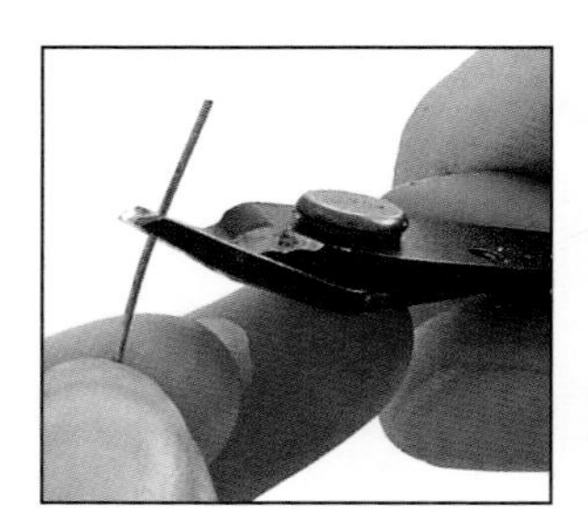

Photo A

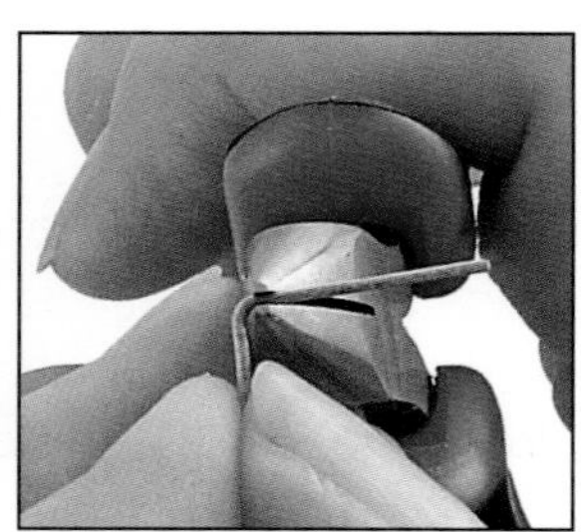

Photo B

Using chain-nose pliers, make a 90-degree bend 3/8 inch from end of wire. (Photo B)

Using round-nose pliers, grasp the end of the wire so no wire sticks out between plier blades. (Photo C1)

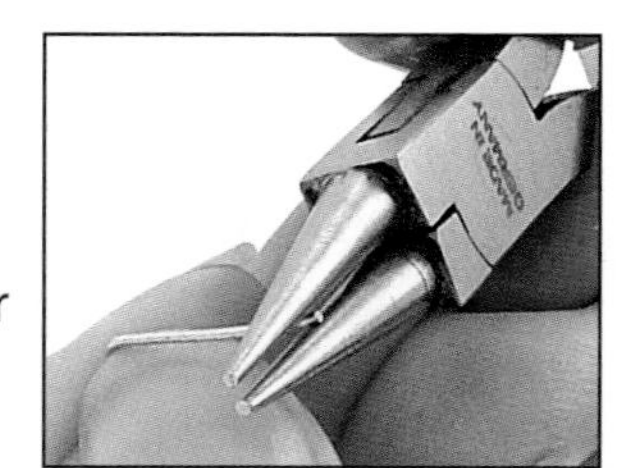

Photo C1

Begin making a loop by rolling your hand away from your body. Don't try to make the entire loop in one movement. Roll your hand ¼ turn counterclockwise. (Photo C2)

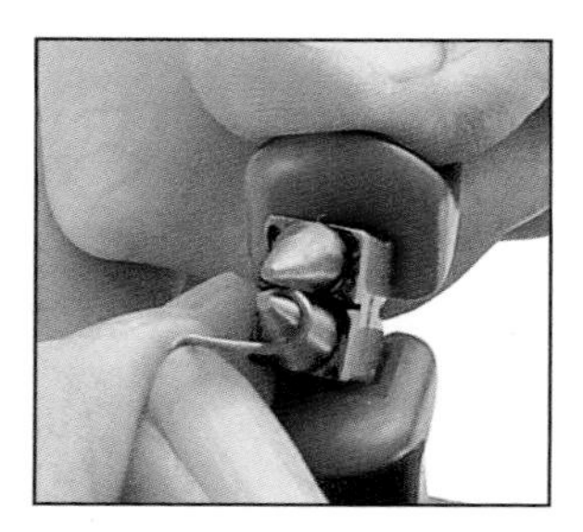

Photo C2

Without removing pliers from loop, open plier blade slightly and pivot plier back toward your body clockwise about ¼ turn. (Photo D)

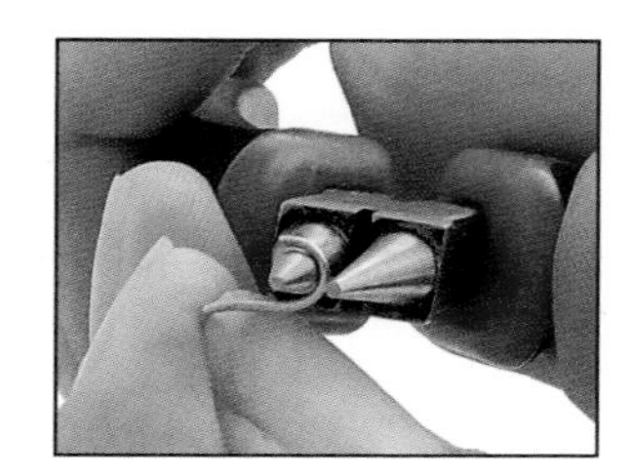

Photo D

Close plier onto the wire and roll the loop until it comes around, next to the 90-degree bend. (Photo E)

Open and close eye-pin loops the same way as jump rings, by pushing open front to back. (Photo F)

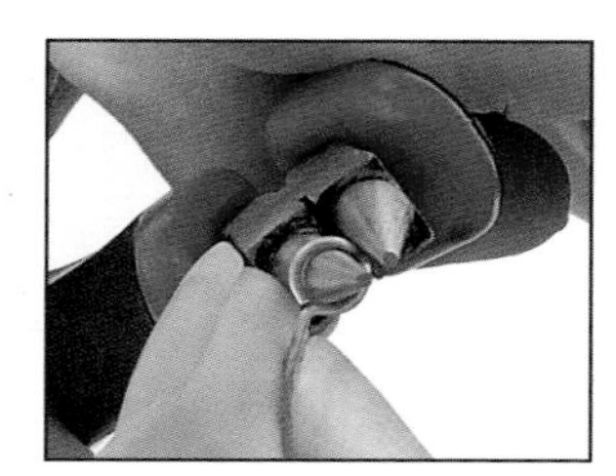

Photo E

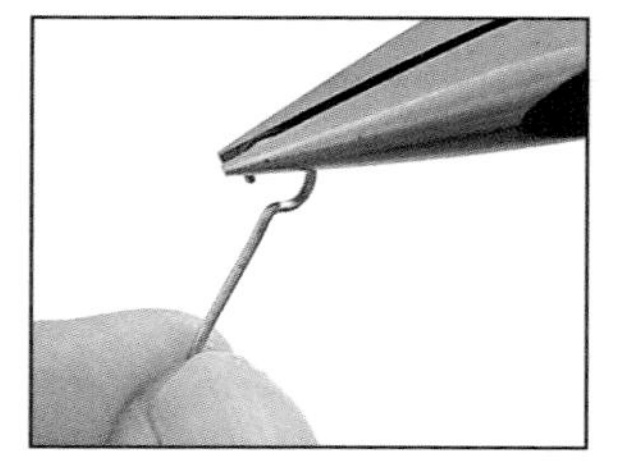

Photo F

MAKING WIRE-WRAPPED LOOPS

Practice wire wrapping with either 22- or 24-gauge wire. Harden slightly by pulling on one end with the other end clamped in a vise or pull one or two times through nylon-jaw pliers. (Photo A)

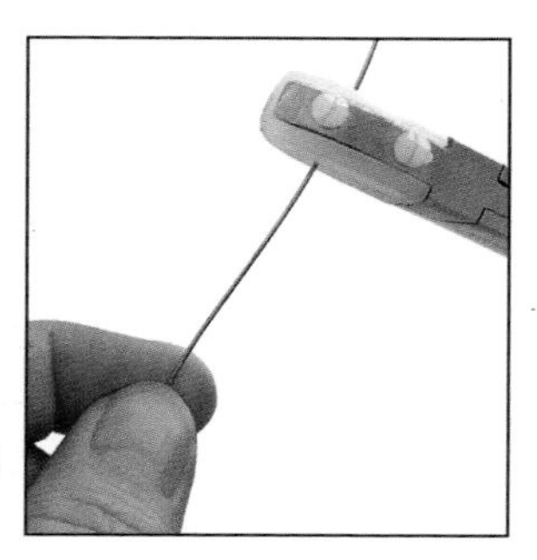

Photo A

Make a 90-degree bend about 1½ inches from end of the wire using chain-nose pliers. (Photo B)

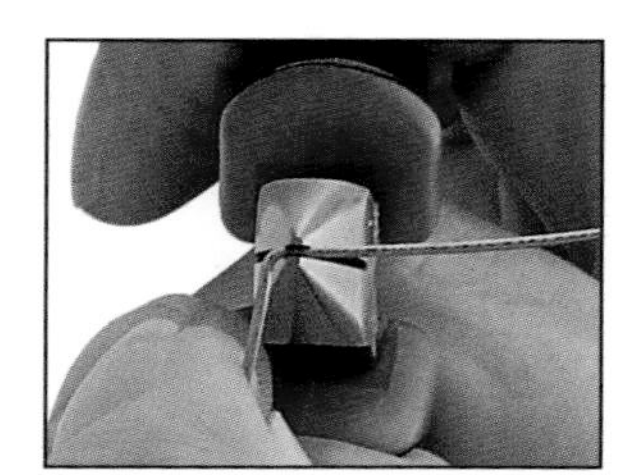

Photo B

Using round-nose pliers, grab wire about ⅜ inch away from the 90-degree and roll your hand away from yourself, toward the bend until a loop is halfway formed. (Photos C1 and C2)

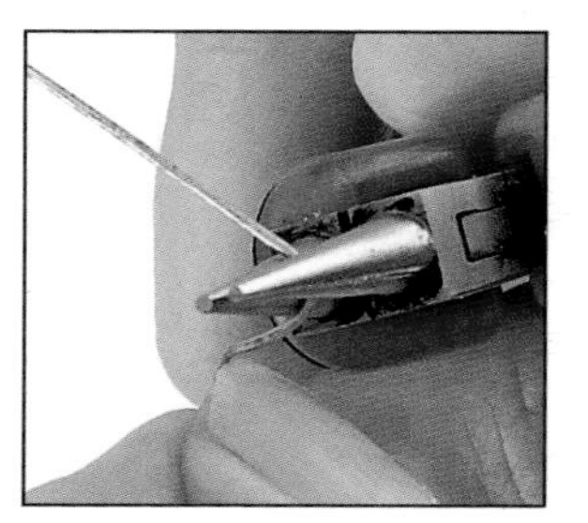

Photo C1

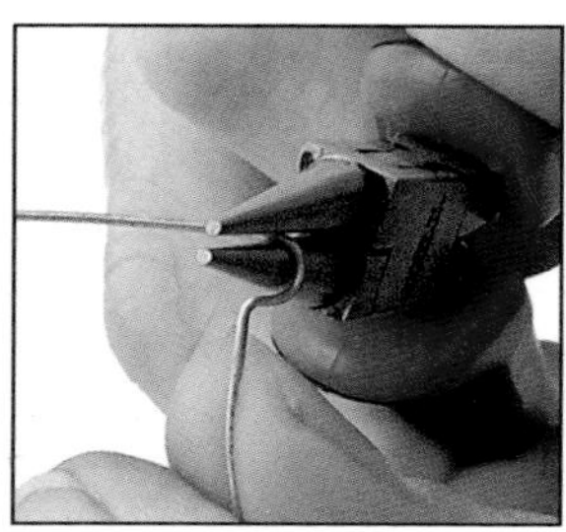

Photo C2

Without removing plier from forming loop, open the jaw and rotate plier clockwise about ¼ turn. (Photo D)

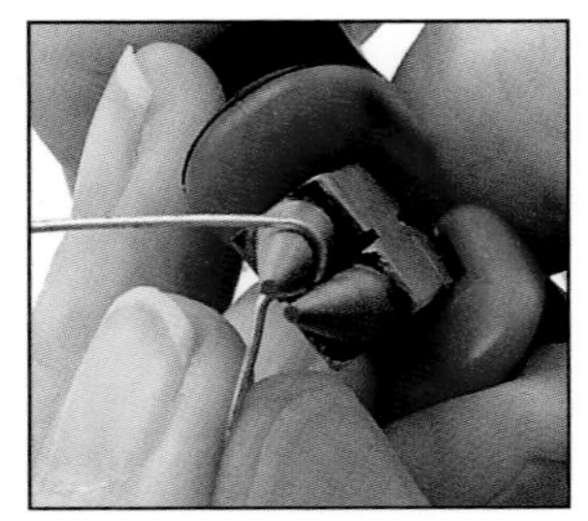

Photo D

Grab the end of the wire with your left (non-dominant) hand and pull it around the rest of the way until it crosses itself and completes the loop. (Photo E)

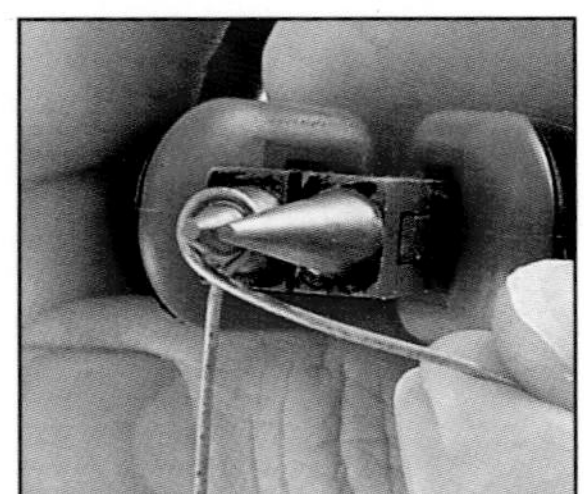

Photo E

Switch to chain-nose pliers, holding across the loop. Wrap tail around wire under loop with your left hand. If you are using a heavy gauge of wire, it is often easier to use a second plier to pull the tail around instead of your fingers. (Photos F1 and F2)

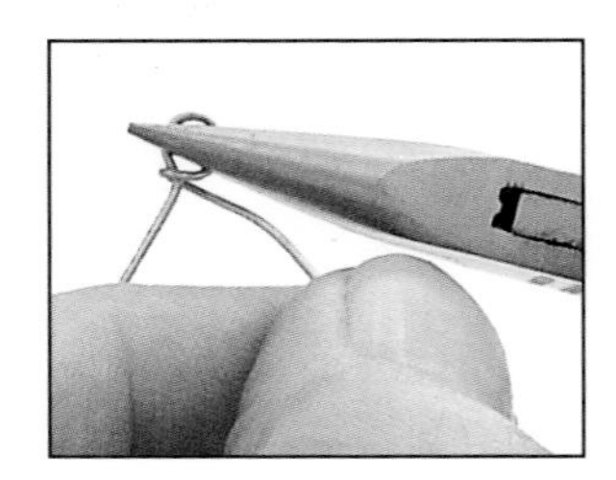

Photo F1

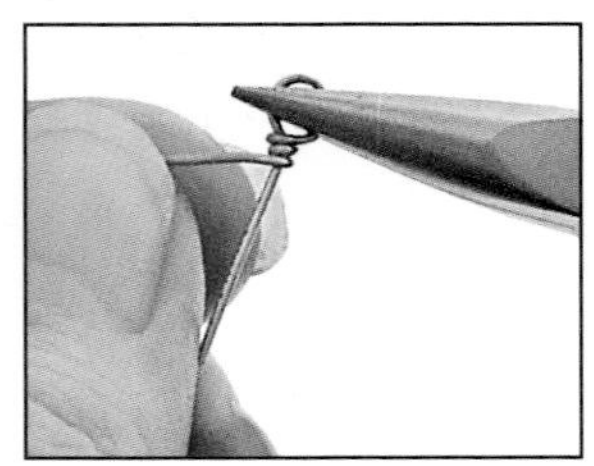

Photo F2

Flush cut wire as close to the wrap as possible. Tuck end down if needed, using chain-nose pliers. (Photos G1 and G2)

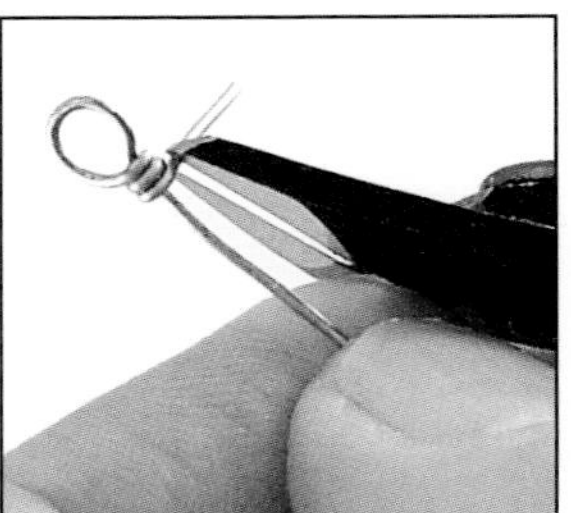

Photo G1

Photo G2

To create a wrap on the opposite end of the bead, leave a gap equal to wrap space on first end. Grasp to the right of the wrap space and make a 90-degree bend. (Photos H1 and H2)

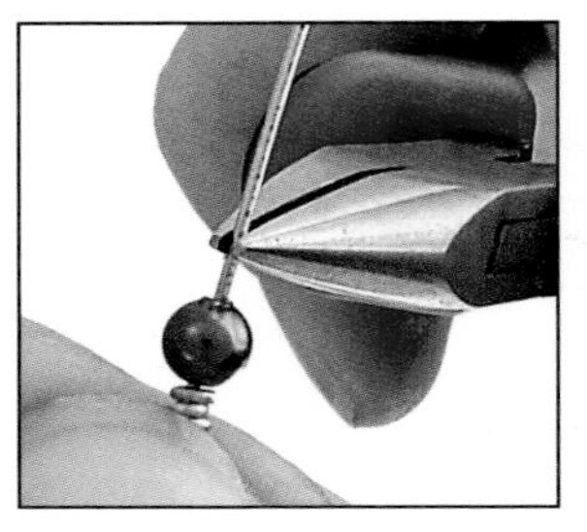

Photo H1

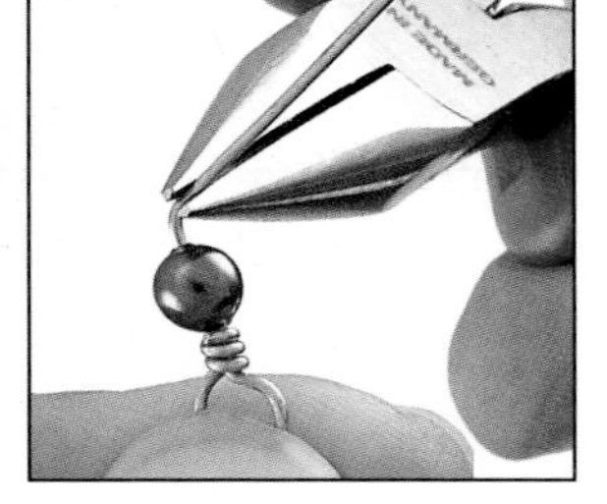

Photo H2

Repeat from Photo C–H to complete.

HAMMERING WIRE

Hammering hardens and flattens round wire. This can be especially important when making ear wires or clasps that need to hold their shape. Always use a smooth, hardened steel surface to guarantee a clean finish. Any marks or scars on a bench block or hammer will impress on the surface of wire or sheet metal.

Create your shape from wire. Keep hammer flat to prevent marring wire. Flip over after a few taps and hammer on opposite side. Don't get carried away, if you hammer too much metal becomes brittle and breaks. (Photo A)

Photo A

CRIMPING

String a crimp bead onto flexible wire. String clasp or ring and pass tail of flexible wire back through crimp to form a loop.

Hold wires parallel and make sure crimp is positioned correctly. Using front slot on plier, shape crimp into a small oval. (Photo A)

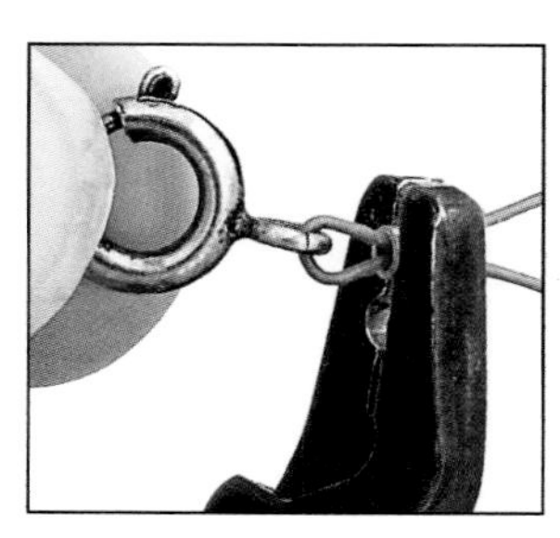

Photo A

Put oval into back slot of plier and squeeze to make fold in the center with one wire on each side of fold. (Photo B)

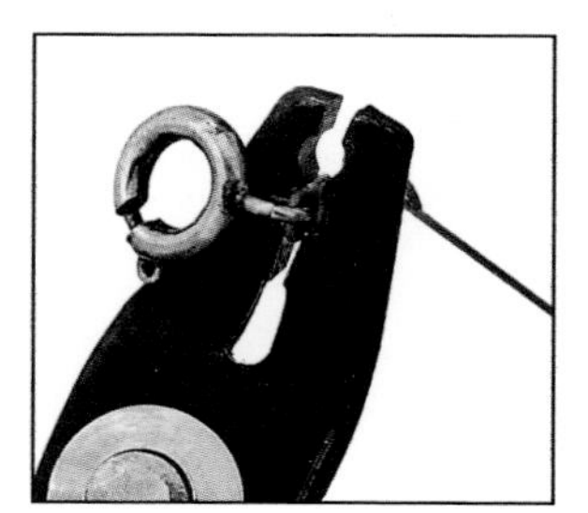

Photo B

Return to front slot, and squeeze again to tighten crimp. Do a few more rotations and squeezes to solidify and shape crimp bead. Trim wire tail. (Photo C)

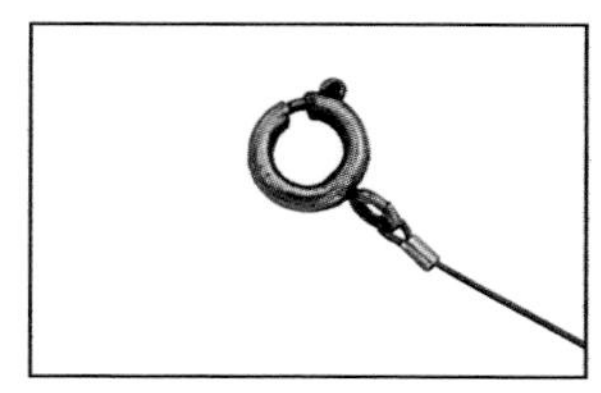

Photo C

hoops & posts

Timeless, easy-to-wear and perfect for jeans, suits or Sunday dresses, hoops and posts are all grown-up and ready to get out of the house. Find a dozen different ways to explore the timeless style of hoops and posts.

intermediate

night fall

Design by Allison Hoffman, courtesy of Fusion Beads

Allison loves working with crystals and wire and what better way to combine the two than these beautiful earrings!

INSTRUCTIONS

1) Starting at one end of hoop, hold one 18-inch wire in your non-dominant hand perpendicular to hoop, leaving approximately 1 inch wire tail. Wrap wire tightly around end of hoop three times to anchor wire.

2) String one crystal and wrap wire around hoop once. Wrap wire around hoop once more making sure wire is as close to previous wrap as possible.

3) Repeat step 2 (15) more times or until you reach end of hoop, leaving approximately ⅛ inch empty at end of hoop.

4) Wrap wire tightly around hoop three times to secure wire to hoop. Trim wire ends.

5) Repeat steps 1–4 for second earring. ●

Source: All materials from Fusion Beads.

MATERIALS

32 (3mm) jet hematite 2x CRYSTALLIZED™ - Swarovski Elements round crystals
2 (2 x 18mm) sterling silver hoops
2 (18-inch) lengths 26-gauge sterling silver dead-soft wire
Flush cutters

FINISHED SIZE

⅞ inch long

easy

garden lantern hoops

Design by Heather Powers

Semi-precious and polymer clay beads illuminate light, bright silver hoops. A perfect pair for an evening in the garden.

INSTRUCTIONS

1) Slide a spacer and a disk bead onto a head pin. Form a loop; trim excess wire. Repeat once.

2) Slide a seed bead and an amazonite rondelle onto a head pin. Form a loop; trim excess wire. Repeat 11 more times.

3) String three amazonite dangles, disk bead dangle and three amazonite dangles onto one hoop. Repeat once.

4) String one crimp bead onto very end of one hoop; use crimp pliers to squeeze gently on the crimp bead to create a stopper. Repeat to complete second earring.

Sources: Branch disk beads from Humblebeads; seed beads from Charlene's Beads.

MATERIALS

2 lime branch disk beads
12 (8mm) amazonite rondelles
12 nickel seed beads
14 (1-inch) sterling silver head pins
2 (4mm) silver spacers
2 (2mm) silver crimp beads
2 (25mm) sterling silver ear hoops
Round-nose pliers
Crimp pliers
Wire nippers

FINISHED SIZE

1¼ inches long

intermediate

wrapped hoops

Design by Fernando Dasilva, courtesy of Fernando Dasilva Jewelry

Like red, hoops are classically stylish. Add romantic yarn, colored wire, crystal sparkle and finish with a dramatic lemon quartz dangle.

INSTRUCTIONS

1) Tie a double knot at one end of one 10-inch length of cotton yarn. Add a dot of cement to knot; let dry.

2) Place knot on flat circle and wrap yarn around circle securing knot in place; continue wrapping yarn until ¼ of circle is covered, making sure wraps are as close as possible. All crystals should be on front of circle. Tie a double knot at end of yarn; add a dot of cement and let dry.

3) Begin wrapping one 10-inch length of red wire around circle at starting point of yarn. Continue wrapping in opposite direction of wrapped yarn until ¼ of circle is covered. Use nylon-jaw pliers to flatten and smooth out wraps as you go. Cut wire and flatten carefully as to not leave a sharp edge.

4) Slide the following onto a head pin: copper AB bicone, bead cap, lemon quartz bead, bead cap, copper AB bicone and a Bead Bumper. ***Note:*** *String bead caps so they "cup" the lemon quartz bead.* Form a loop approximately ¼ inch above Bead Bumper; trim excess wire.

5) Open a jump ring and attach to hole at top of flat circle and loop on ear post; close ring.

6) Open loop on beaded head pin from step 4 and slide onto jump ring from step 5; close loop.

7) Repeat steps 1–6 for second earring. ●

Sources: Lemon quartz beads from Bijoux Collection; bead caps, jump rings, head pins, Bead Bumpers and ColourCraft wire from Beadalon; flat circle doughnuts and sterling silver ear posts from Fernando Dasilva Jewelry; bicone crystals and cotton yarn from CRYSTALLIZED™ - Swarovski Elements.

MATERIALS

4 (3mm) copper AB CRYSTALLIZED™ - Swarovski Elements bicone crystals
2 (18 x 14mm) faceted lemon quartz oval beads
4 gold-plated bead caps
2 (2mm) clear oval Bead Bumpers
2 gold-plated ball-tip head pins
2 (6mm) sterling silver round jump rings
2 (1¾-inch) silver-plated polished flat circle doughnuts
2 sterling silver rectangle modern ear posts
2 (10-inch) lengths CRYSTALLIZED™ - Swarovski Elements copper cotton yarn with 3mm copper crystals
2 (10-inch) lengths 24-gauge red wire
Round-nose pliers
Chain-nose pliers
Nylon-jaw pliers
Flush cutters
Jewelry cement

FINISHED SIZE

2¼ inches long

intermediate

oceans of delight

Design by Margot Potter

These flirty earrings will be your 'go to' summertime pair. Freshwater pearls, apatite and rutilated quartz cascade from sterling hoops for an enchanting effect. Fit for a mermaid, made to fit you.

INSTRUCTIONS

1) String a crimp tube onto hoop and slide it up against receptive end of hoop. Use chain-nose pliers to flatten and secure tube in place with chain-nose pliers. This will prevent beaded dangles from falling off. Repeat for second hoop.

2) Slide a bead onto a head pin; form a wrapped loop. Trim excess wire. Repeat for each head pin.

3) Slide beaded dangles onto hoop as follows: pearl, rutilated quartz and apatite. Repeat three more times; slide on a pearl and rutilated quartz. Repeat for second earring.

4) Flatten and secure a crimp tube approximately ⅛ inch from insertion end of hoop. Repeat for second earring.

5) Use round-pliers to bend wire end on each hoop up at a 90-degree angle to secure earrings closed when wearing. ●

Sources: Apatite nuggets from Bead Trust; freshwater pearls and rutilated quartz coins fron Wonder Sources Inc.; findings from Marvin Schwab/The Bead Warehouse.

MATERIALS

8 (8mm) freeform apatite nuggets

8 (6mm) cream freshwater pearls

8 (8mm) rutilated quartz coins

24 (24-gauge) sterling silver head pins

4 (2 x 2mm) sterling silver crimp tubes

2 (1¼-inch) sterling silver hoops

Round-nose pliers

2 pairs chain-nose pliers

Wire nippers

FINISHED SIZE

1⅞ inches long

hoopla

Design by Rupa Balachandar

These hoop earrings create a visual treat because of the alternating drops of turquoise and coral beads. When worn with a plain white shirt and denim, these earrings will add much-needed pizzazz.

INSTRUCTIONS

1) Slide a coral bead and a turquoise bead on a head pin. Form a loop; trim excess wire. Repeat nine more times for a total of 10 dangles. These will be referred to as A dangles.

2) Slide a turquoise bead and a coral bead on a head pin. Form a loop; trim excess wire. Repeat seven more times for a total of eight dangles. These will be referred to as B dangles.

3) Open loop on an A dangle slightly and attach to first loop on an ear hoop; close loop. Open loop on a B dangle and attach to second loop on ear hoop; close loop. Continue attaching dangles to ear hoop, alternating A and B dangles until all loops are filled.

4) Repeat step 3 to complete second earring. ●

Source: Beads and ear hoops from RupaB Designs.

MATERIALS

4–5mm round beads: 18 coral, 18 reconstituted turquoise

18 (1-inch) gold head pins

2 (55mm) gold-filled 9-loop ear hoops

Round-nose pliers

Chain-nose pliers

Wire nippers

FINISHED SIZE

2¾ inches long

easy

sassy sequin hoops

Design by Alexa Westerfield

These sassy earrings are easy to make and perfect for people of just about every age! Lightweight, a little sparkly and all fun!

INSTRUCTIONS

1) Cut off two large sequins, four medium sequins, four small sequins and four tiny sequins from fringe.

2) String the following on a hoop, stringing a silver bead between each: tiny sequin, small sequin, medium sequin, large sequin, medium sequin, small sequin and tiny sequin.

3) Using pliers, bend back end of hoop approximately ⅛ inch. Insert end into hoop to close.

4) Open loop on ear wire and slide on loop on hoop; close loop.

5) Repeat steps 2–4 for second earring.

Sources: Sequin fringe from Wal-Mart Stores Inc.; silver-plated beads, hoops and ear wires from Michaels Stores Inc.

MATERIALS

Sequin beaded fringe with 4 different sizes of sequins
12 (4mm) silver-plated round beads
2 silver hoops
2 silver-plated ear wires
Chain-nose pliers

FINISHED SIZE

2¼ inches long

easy

sassy silkies posts

Design by Kristal Wick, courtesy of Sassy Silkies

Ancient-looking coins and silk cylinders with a central dot of crystal sit solidly atop traditional post earring backs. Change colors, coins or shapes for a little variation.

INSTRUCTIONS

1) Glue a scroll bead to front of one coin covering the hole. Let dry. Repeat for second coin.

2) Glue a crystal to each scroll bead; let dry.

3) Flip coins over and glue post backs to backs of coins. Let dry. Repeat for second earring.

Sources: Coins from Rings & Things; Sassy Silky beads from Sassy Silkies/Kristal Wick; CRYSTALLIZED™ - Swarovski Elements from Fusion Beads; earring backs and stoppers from Artbeads.com.

MATERIALS

2 (1-inch-diameter) gold Asian coins

2 (1-inch) medium Sassy Silky scroll beads

2 flat-back CRYSTALLIZED™ - Swarovski Elements

2 post earring backs & stoppers

Glue

FINISHED SIZE

1 inch diameter

easy

urban jungle

Design by Camilla Jorgensen

Dressed down with your favorite pair of worn-out jeans, or dressed up with an 80s inspired gold mesh mini dress, these multifunctional earrings are sure to cause quite a stir!

INSTRUCTIONS

1) Slide a lime crystal onto a head pin; form a loop. Trim excess wire. Repeat for each crystal and freshwater pearl for a total of 24 dangles.

2) Open loop on a pearl dangle and attach to end link of one chain length; close loop. In the same manner, attach a crystal dangle to next link, a pearl dangle to next link and so on until there are six pearl dangles and six crystal dangles attached to chain. Repeat once.

3) Cut off excess chain attached to toggle bars. ***Note:*** *Leave one chain link attached to each toggle bar.*

4) Use both pairs of pliers to open one jump ring and attach to toggle bar; slide jump ring through loop on top crystal dangle on one chain before closing.

5) Open loop on an earring stud and slide onto round half of toggle clasp; close loop. Insert toggle bar with attached dangles through round half of toggle.

6) Repeat steps 4 and 5 for second earring.

Sources: CRYSTALLIZED™ - Swarovski Elements bicone crystals, jump rings, earring studs and chain from Frabels Inc.; clasps from Nina Designs.

MATERIALS

12 (6mm) lime CRYSTALLIZED™-Swarovski Elements bicone crystals
12 (6mm) lime freshwater pearls
24 (½-inch) sterling silver head pins
2 (4mm) sterling silver jump rings
2 (10mm) sterling silver earring studs
2 (18 x 15mm) sterling silver toggle clasps
2 (⅞-inch) lengths 2mm oval sterling silver chain
Round-nose pliers
Flat-nose pliers
Flush cutters

FINISHED SIZE

2 inches long

intermediate

rustic essence

Design by Laura Stafford, courtesy of Tucson Mountain Jewelry

Shining crystal and subtle faceted tiger's-eye beads make a high-contrast combination. Decorative head pins finish the bottom of the earring with an extra punch of texture and a flash of silver.

INSTRUCTIONS

1) String the following on a head pin: sterling silver bead, tiger's-eye bead, clear crystal and tiger's-eye bead. Form a wrapped loop, attaching loop to ring on ball post before wrapping. Trim excess wire.

2) Repeat step 1 for second earring. ●

Sources: Tiger's-eye beads from Earthstone; sterling silver beads from Jayamahe Bali; CRYSTALLIZED™ - Swarovski Elements, head pins and sterling silver ball posts from Fusion Beads.

MATERIALS

2 (11mm) sterling silver Bali-style beads
4 (8mm) faceted tiger's-eye beads
2 (4mm) clear bicone CRYSTALLIZED™ - Swarovski Elements
2 sterling silver head pins
2 (4mm) sterling silver ball posts with ring
Round-nose pliers
Chain-nose pliers
Wire nippers

FINISHED SIZE

1¾ inches long

easy

starbursts

Design by Camilla Jorgensen

Light, romantic and fun, sterling silver earrings sparkle with crystal accents. AB-finished crystals give a rainbow of fiery contrast to shiny hammered accents.

INSTRUCTIONS

1) Slide a light sapphire crystal onto a head pin. Form a loop above crystal; trim excess wire. Repeat for each crystal.

2) Use both pairs of chain-nose pliers to open a jump ring. Slide seven beaded head pins and one hammered oval (convex side out) onto ring; close jump ring.

3) Open another jump ring and slide on seven beaded head pins and another hammered oval (convex side out); slide jump ring through top hole of hammered oval from step 2. Close ring.

4) Open another jump ring and slide on seven beaded head pins; slide jump ring through top hole of second hammered oval and loop on ear stud. Close jump ring.

5) Repeat steps 2–4 for second earring. ●

Sources: CRYSTALLIZED™ - Swarovski Elements bicone crystals and sterling silver findings from Frabels Inc.; sterling silver hammered ovals from Somerset Silver Inc.

MATERIALS

42 (4mm) light sapphire AB2X CRYSTALLIZED™-Swarovski Elements bicone crystals

4 (8 x 14mm) sterling silver 2-hole hammered oval links

42 (½-inch) sterling silver ball-tip head pins

6 (5mm) sterling silver jump rings

2 (8mm) sterling silver hammered earring studs

Round-nose pliers

2 pairs of chain-nose pliers

Flush cutters

FINISHED SIZE

2 inches long

intermediate

royal elegance

Design by Laura Stafford, courtesy of Tucson Mountain Jewelry

These nearly weightless post earrings will make you feel like royalty. Stunning blue is perfect with jeans or something a bit more dressed up.

INSTRUCTIONS

1) String the following on a head pin: Capri blue crystal, cinnabar bead and a Capri blue crystal. Form a wrapped loop, attaching loop to earring before wrapping. Trim excess wire. Repeat once.

Sources: Cinnabar beads from Fire Mountain Gems and Beads; CRYSTALLIZED™ - Swarovski Elements bicone crystals and head pins from Fusion Beads; Bali-style earrings from Brightlings Beads.

MATERIALS
2 blue imitation cinnabar floral beads
4 (4mm) Capri blue CRYSTALLIZED™-Swarovski Elements bicone crystals
2 sterling silver head pins
2 (7mm) silver Bali-style earrings with drop
Round-nose pliers
Chain-nose pliers
Wire nippers

FINISHED SIZE
1⅝ inches long

easy

beach fun

Design by Camilla Jorgensen

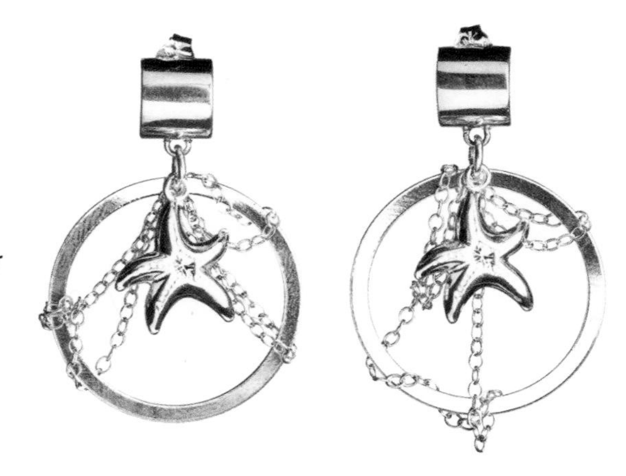

Light, romantic and fun, these sterling silver earrings will have you thinking of sunny spring afternoons spent strolling along the beach without a care in the world.

INSTRUCTIONS

1) Use both pairs of pliers to open one jump ring. Slide one end of one 6-inch chain onto jump ring; randomly wrap chain around one sterling silver open ring. Thread jump ring through hole at top of open ring; attach end of chain to jump ring.

2) Slide one starfish onto jump ring. Thread jump ring through loop on ear stud. Close ring.

3) Repeat steps 1 and 2 for second earring.

Source: All materials from Fire Mountain Gems and Beads.

MATERIALS

2 (13mm) sterling silver starfish charms

2 (5mm) sterling silver jump rings

2 (27mm) sterling silver open rings with 1 hole

2 (8mm) sterling silver hammered square earring studs

2 (6-inch) lengths 2mm oval sterling silver chain

Round-nose pliers

Flat-nose pliers

Flush cutters

FINISHED SIZE

1½ inches long

short dangles

Face the facts—short dangles (under 2 inches) are the backbone of every great earring collection. Go from subtle to bold and back again in any one of 25 short and sassy earring designs.

easy

fabric love

Design by Candie Cooper

Your Gram's tattered apron or that fabulous bag of retro quilting scraps—both are the perfect start to making these unique earrings.

INSTRUCTIONS

1) Use charms as templates to cut two pieces from fabric.

2) Apply a layer of decoupage medium on back of a clear charm with foam brush. Press charm on top of one fabric piece and press down; burnish fabric on back so there are no air bubbles. Repeat once. Set aside to dry.

3) Use awl or large needle to poke a hole at center top of each charm.

4) Open a jump ring and slide on a flower charm; slide jump ring through fabric charm. Close ring.

5) String a few beads on an eye pin; form a loop. Trim excess wire. Open one loop and attach to jump ring attached to charm; close loop.

6) Repeat steps 4 and 5 for second earring.

7) Open loops on ear wires and slide on top loops of dangles; close loops. ●

Source: Clear glass square tags, jump rings and decoupage medium from Plaid Enterprises Inc.

MATERIALS:

Printed fabric
Beads
2 silver flower spacer beads or brass flower charms
2 clear charms or tags
2 silver eye pins
2 jump rings
2 ear wires
Round-nose pliers
Chain-nose pliers
Wire nippers
Awl or large embroidery needle
Small foam brush
Decoupage medium

FINISHED SIZE

2 inches long

easy

beautiful flight

Design by Jeanne Holland, courtesy of Vintaj Natural Brass Co.

Filigree, flowers and butterflies adorn your ears for the perfect summer earrings!

INSTRUCTIONS

1) String one teal fire-polished bead, foliage bead cap and chartreuse flower bead onto a head pin. ***Note:*** *String bead cap so it "cups" the fire-polished bead.* Form a loop, attaching loop to a 7.25mm jump ring before closing. Trim excess wire.

2) Use a 4.75mm jump ring to attach a butterfly charm to 7.25mm jump ring from step 1. Set aside.

3) Using round-nose pliers, carefully bend wings of one filigree butterfly connector to create a setting for one navette stone. Slide stone into setting, using chain-nose pliers to crimp edges of filigree wings to secure stone in place.

4) Attach a 4.75mm jump ring through 7.25mm jump ring containing beaded dangle and charm. String 4.75mm jump ring through bottom opening of filigree wing; close ring to secure.

5) Open loop on ear wire and slide through top opening of filigree wing; close loop.

6) Repeat steps 1–5 for second earring.

Sources: Natural brass components (wholesale) from Vintaj Natural Brass Co.; all other beads and natural brass components (retail) from Galena Beads.

MATERIALS

2 (4mm) teal fire-polished round beads

2 (7 x 12mm) chartreuse German glass bell flower beads

2 (9 x 18mm) topaz marquise cut navette stones

2 (16 x 16mm) filigree butterfly connectors

2 (9 x 11mm) natural brass teensie butterfly charms

2 (8mm) natural brass foliage bead caps

Natural brass jump rings: 2 (7.25mm), 4 (4.75mm)

2 (1-inch) 21-gauge natural brass head pins

2 (20 x 15mm) natural brass round loop ear wires

Round-nose pliers

Chain-nose pliers

Flush cutters

FINISHED SIZE

2¼ inches long

crystal stash

Design by Margot Potter

These tiny glass vials hold a small stash of crystal beads. Pretty colors of pink, gray and black combine with gold findings and make a whimsical yet elegant effect. It's easy to switch up the beads on the inside if your mood or your outfit changes.

INSTRUCTIONS

1) Fill vials with four jet crystals, four crystal vitrial AB crystals and five light rose AB crystals, alternating colors as you fill. Seal vial, using glue to permanently seal vial if desired.

2) Slide a crystal on a head pin; form a wrapped loop. Trim excess wire. Repeat for each remaining crystal for a total of six beaded dangles.

3) Open a jump ring and slide on one of each color of dangle; close ring. Repeat once.

4) Open loop at top of vial using chain-nose pliers. Slide beaded jump ring and ear wire on loop; close loop. Repeat once.

5) Turn eyes of ear wires so earrings are facing forward using chain-nose pliers to adjust.

Sources: Glass vials from ARTchix Studio; crystals from CRYSTALLIZED™ - Swarovski Elements; findings from Beadalon.

MATERIALS:

3mm CRYSTALLIZED™-Swarovski Elements round crystals: 10 jet, 12 light rose AB, 10 crystal vitrial AB
2 (1½-inch) clear test-tube glass vials
2 (4mm) gold-plated jump rings
6 gold-plated head pins
2 gold-plated ear wires
Round-nose pliers
2 pairs of chain-nose pliers
Wire nippers
Jeweler's glue (optional)

FINISHED SIZE

2 inches long

feelin' the blues

Design by Alexa Westerfield

These blue beauties are perfect for dressing up with a fancy top or down with your favorite jeans.

INSTRUCTIONS

1) String the following on a head pin: cat's-eye bead, spacer, disk, spacer and cat's-eye bead. Form a loop; attach loop to end link of one 1-inch chain before closing. Trim excess wire. Repeat once.

2) Open loops on ear wires and attach to end links of chains; close loops.

Sources: Light blue disk beads, spacers and chain from Michaels Stores Inc.; blue cat's-eye beads from Darice Inc.

MATERIALS

2 (16mm) light blue transparent disk beads
4 (4mm) blue cat's-eye beads
4 (4mm) silver-plated daisy spacers
2 silver-plated head pins
2 (1-inch) pieces silver chain
Round-nose pliers
Wire nippers

FINISHED SIZE

2¾ inches long

intermediate

egyptian earrings

Design by Liz Revit, courtesy of E.A. Revit Inc.

Simple yet elegant, these earrings were inspired by the designs of ancient Egypt. Learn how to make these fabulous earrings by using cold-join techniques.

Project note: *When forging wire, gently hammer it, then guide the hammer away from the wire to create a flared look.*

INSTRUCTIONS

1) Using hammer and steel bench block, gently forge each end of one ¾-inch wire. Set aside.

2) To create horseshoe-shaped component, use fingers to gently bend one 1½-inch wire in half. Use round-nose pliers to form a loop on each side of wire. Before closing loops, slip one forged piece of wire from step 1 into loops; center forged wire below horseshoe. Close loops tightly so they grip the forged wire.

3) To hold forged wire in place, wrap a 1-inch piece of 24-gauge wire around forged wire on outside of horseshoe. Repeat for other side of earring.

4) To create tiny loop at top of horseshoe, bend a 2-inch wire in half using round-nose pliers. Center loop behind top of horseshoe; wrap loose ends of wire around both sides of horseshoe. Attach ear wire to this loop.

5) To create forged head pins, gently forge one end of one 1-inch 20-gauge wire and two ¾-inch wires in the same manner as in step 1.

6) String the following onto 1-inch head pin: lined pale peach AB seed bead, pacific opal bicone and a lined pale peach AB seed bead. Form a loop above top bead. Before closing loop, attach it to bottom of earring.

7) String the following onto each ¾-inch head pin: transparent light amber AB seed bead, padparadscha bicone and a transparent light amber AB seed bead. Form a loop above top bead. Before closing loop, attach it to bottom of earring. Repeat once and attach to other side of 1-inch dangle on earring.

8) Repeat steps 1–7 for second earring.

Sources: CRYSTALLIZED™ - Swarovski Elements bicone crystals, ear wires and sterling silver wire from Fusion Beads; Miyuki Delicas from Clearwater Beads.

MATERIALS

4mm CRYSTALLIZED™ - Swarovski Elements bicone crystals:
 4 padparadscha,
 2 pacific opal

10/0 Delica seed beads: 8 transparent light amber AB, 4 lined pale peach AB

2 sterling silver ear wires

24-gauge sterling silver dead soft wire: 4 (1-inch) pieces, 2 (2-inch) pieces

20-gauge sterling silver dead soft wire: 6 (¾-inch) pieces, 2 (1-inch) pieces, 2 (1½-inch) pieces

Ball peen hammer

Steel bench block

Round-nose pliers

Chain-nose pliers

Flat-nose pliers

Wire nippers

FINISHED SIZE

1¾ inches long

easy

cindi

Design by Molly Schaller

Breezy, with a sunny disposition and a flair for the dramatic, Cindi loves the basics. Cindi looks great with any outfit.

INSTRUCTIONS

1) Slide an onyx round bead and a bead cap onto an eye pin. ***Note:*** *String bead cap so it "cups" the onyx bead.* Form a loop; trim excess wire. Repeat once.

2) Open top loops of eye pins and attach to loops on ear wires; close loops.

3) Open bottom loops of eye pins and slide each onto silver rings; close loops.

Sources: Onyx beads, silver rings and ear wires from Fire Mountain Gems and Beads; bead caps from Shiana.

MATERIALS

2 (8mm) onyx round beads
2 (7mm) silver flower bead caps
2 (12mm) silver rings
2 (1-inch) silver eye pins
2 silver ear wires
Round-nose pliers
Chain-nose pliers
Flush cutters

FINISHED SIZE

1½ inches long

intermediate

relique earrings

Design by Kristal Wick, courtesy of Sassy Silkies

Ink stamps turn simple brass circles into ancient-looking treasures. Black crystals and metallic-colored crystals finish the perfect illusion of found jewels.

INSTRUCTIONS

1) Stamp swirls on one side of each brass dangle; let dry. Stamp other sides of dangles; let dry.

2) Open loop of eye pin and attach to top loop of one brass dangle; close loop.

3) String a crystal copper bicone, smoked topaz bicone, crystal copper round, smoked topaz bicone and a crystal copper bicone onto eye pin. Form a loop above top crystal. Trim excess wire.

4) Slide loop onto ear wire. String a black bicone, light Colorado topaz bicone and a black bicone on ear wire.

5) Follow manufacturer's instructions to use epoxy to glue a crystal onto bottom of brass dangle. Let cure 24 hours.

6) Repeat steps 2–5 for second earring.

Sources: CRYSTALLIZED™ - Swarovski Elements crystals from Fusion Beads; brass dangles from Unit Tool Co.; findings from Artbeads.com; stamp from Clearsnap Inc.; solvent ink pad from Tsukineko Inc.

MATERIALS

CRYSTALLIZED™ - Swarovski Elements bicone crystals: 4 (3mm) black, 4 (3mm) crystal copper, 4 (4mm) smoked topaz, 2 (4mm) light Colorado topaz
2 (8mm) crystal copper CRYSTALLIZED™ - Swarovski Elements round crystals
2 brass circle dangles
2 crystal copper CRYSTALLIZED™ - Swarovski Elements flat-back crystals
2 gold eye pins
2 gold kidney ear wires
Swirl stamp
Black solvent-based ink pad
Round-nose pliers
Chain-nose pliers
Wire nippers
Toothpick
2-part epoxy

FINISHED SIZE

2⅜ inches long

easy

hyacinth honey

Design by Rupa Balachandar

This pair of earrings with the delicate floral dangles studded with crystals are easy to create and will always look gorgeous.

INSTRUCTIONS

1) Open one jump ring and slide it onto one of the loops on back of peach/hyacinth flower and one loop of hyacinth drop; close ring. Repeat once.

2) Open loops on ear wires and slide on top loops of hyacinth drops; close loops.

Source: Flower components and ear wires from RupaB Designs.

MATERIALS

2 (10mm) hyacinth CRYSTALLIZED™ - Swarovski Elements 2-loop floral drops

2 (10mm) peach/hyacinth CRYSTALLIZED™ - Swarovski Elements five-petal flowers

2 (5mm) antique-finish jump rings

2 antique gold-finish lever-back ear wires

Flat-nose pliers

Chain-nose pliers

FINISHED SIZE

2 inches long

intermediate

juxt

Design by Jenna Colyar-Cooper, courtesy of Fusion Beads

Shell is a great material for summer jewelry and who doesn't love a little crystal bling? The unique frame shell pendants inspired Jenna to create these fun summer earrings!

INSTRUCTIONS

1) String eight crystals on one head pin. Form a wrapped loop; trim excess wire.

2) Open one jump ring and slide on shell frame link and beaded head pin; close jump ring.

3) Open another jump ring and attach to jump ring from step 2; slide jump ring onto loop on ear wire before closing.

4) Repeat steps 1–3 for second earring.

Source: All materials from Fusion Beads.

MATERIALS

16 (4mm) smoked topaz CRYSTALLIZED™ - Swarovski Elements bicone crystals
2 (10 x 36mm) mother-of-pearl shell rectangular frame links
4 (5.8mm) gold-filled jump rings
2 (2-inch) 24-gauge gold-filled head pins
2 (22mm) gold-filled ear wires with 2mm bead
Round-nose pliers
Chain-nose pliers
Flush cutters

FINISHED SIZE

2⅛ inches long

intermediate

sweet medley

Design by Laura Stafford, courtesy of Tucson Mountain Jewelry

These earrings will complement that special outfit with a mix of delicate cloisonné and contrasting Bali silver caps.

INSTRUCTIONS

1) String the following on a head pin: emerald green bicone, bead cap, cloisonné bead, bead cap and an emerald green bicone. ***Note:*** *String bead caps so they "cup" the cloisonné bead.* Form a wrapped loop; trim excess wire. Repeat once.

2) Open loops on ear wires and attach beaded head pins; close loops.

Sources: Cloisonné beads from Fire Mountain Gems and Beads; bead caps and head pins from Brightlings Beads.

MATERIALS

2 (15 x 25mm) cloisonné oval beads

4 (4mm) emerald green CRYSTALLIZED™-Swarovski Elements bicone crystals

4 (4 x 12.5mm) silver Bali bead caps

2 (2½-inch) sterling silver Bali-style head pins

2 sterling silver ear wires with open loop

Round-nose pliers

Chain-nose pliers

Wire nippers

FINISHED SIZE

2½ inches long

kaia's dream

Design by Molly Schaller

Simple ceramic and wooden beads balance perfectly with silver-plated disks. Dream on.

INSTRUCTIONS

1) Onto one head pin, slide one silver disk, one Kazuri bead and one wooden round. Form a loop; trim excess wire.

2) Use chain-nose pliers to open loop and attach to ear wire; close loop.

3) Repeat steps 1 and 2 for second earring.

Sources: Kazuri beads from Kazuri West; silver disks from Halcraft USA; wooden round beads from Fusion Beads; head pins from Beadalon.

MATERIALS

2 (8mm) Nangka wooden round beads
2 (20 x 20mm) sky blue ceramic Kazuri beads
2 (5mm) silver-plated disks
2 (2-inch) silver head pins
2 silver ear wires
Round-nose pliers
Chain-nose pliers
Flush cutters

FINISHED SIZE

2 inches long

easy

triumvirate

Design by Barb Switzer

Dramatic textured ear wires and royal green drops make a simple earring look like expensive jewelry from a glass case. These dressy drops drape beautifully, with a hint of delicate movement.

INSTRUCTIONS

1) Cut two pieces of chain, each three links long.

2) Use both pairs of pliers to open a 4mm jump ring; slide ring onto end link of one chain and attach to ear-wire loop. Close ring.

3) Use a 5mm jump ring to attach large briolette to end link of chain.

4) Use a 4mm jump ring to attach a smaller briolette to center link of chain. Repeat on opposite side of same chain link.

5) Repeat steps 2–4 for second earring.

Source: All materials available from Fusion Beads.

MATERIALS

Palace green CRYSTALLIZED™-Swarovski Elements briolettes: 4 (11 x 5.5mm), 2 (13 x 6.5mm)

Sterling silver jump rings: 6 (4mm), 2 (5mm)

2 (44 x 20mm) silver textured ear wires

1 inch sterling silver flat oval link chain

2 pairs chain-nose pliers

Flush cutters

FINISHED SIZE

2 inches long

easy

shell earrings

Design by Helen Rafson

White is essential, pure and goes with everything. Beautiful coin shell beads are stunning with a dash of small beads and shining silver.

INSTRUCTIONS

1) String the following onto a head pin: silver round bead, silver spacer, white shell coin, silver spacer, silver round bead, 10 white seed beads and a silver round bead. Form a loop. Trim excess wire. Repeat once.

2) Open loops on ear wires and slide on beaded head pins.

Source: Silver spacers from Hirschberg Schutz & Co. Inc.

MATERIALS

2 (15mm) white shell coin beads
6 (3mm) silver round beads
20 white seed beads
4 silver spacers
2 silver head pins
2 silver French ear wires
Round-nose pliers
Chain-nose pliers
Wire nippers

FINISHED SIZE

2½ inches long

easy

dangling by a thread

Designs by Laurie D'Ambrosio

Make elegant earrings in a snap with a few small lightweight beads. The threader findings make it simple to add a few dangles. Change the length of the earring by pulling more of the chain through to the back.

INSTRUCTIONS

1) Slide a black round, fuchsia round and a black round on a head pin. Form a loop; trim excess wire. Repeat once.

2) Slide a crystal AB bicone on a head pin. Form a loop; trim excess wire. Repeat three more times.

3) Open loops on two crystal AB dangles and attach to loop on an ear thread; close loops. Open loop on one black/fuchsia dangle and slide onto one of the crystal AB dangle loops attached to ear thread. Close loop.

4) Repeat step 3 for second earring. ●

Sources: Bicone crystals from CRYSTALLIZED™ - Swarovski Elements; ear threads and head pins from Cousin Corp. of America.

MATERIALS

4 (4mm) crystal AB CRYSTALLIZED™-Swarovski Elements bicone crystals
Round beads: 2 (6mm) fuchsia, 4 (4mm) black
6 (1-inch) sterling silver head pins
2 sterling silver ear threads
Round-nose pliers
Chain-nose pliers
Wire nippers

FINISHED SIZE

3¼ inches long

intermediate

bubble bead

Design by Annie Destito, courtesy of Glass Bead Store

Show off handmade glass beads with caps and ear wires. These bubble beauties are simple enough to dress up, dress down or go with all your favorite tops.

INSTRUCTIONS

1) Slide a seed bead, bead cap, three to five seed beads, bubble bead (which will slide over the seed beads), bead cap and a seed bead on a head pin. ***Note:*** *String bead caps so they "cup" the bubble bead.* Form a wrapped loop; trim excess wire. Repeat once.

2) Open ear-wire loops and slide on beaded dangles; close loops.

Sources: Bubble beads from Glass Bead Store; ear wires, head pins and bead caps from Fire Mountain Gems and Beads.

MATERIALS

2 lampwork glass bubble beads
10–14 (11/0) seed beads to match
4 sterling silver flower-shaped bead caps
2 sterling silver head pins
2 sterling silver ear wires
Round-nose pliers
Chain-nose pliers
Wire nippers

FINISHED SIZE

1½ inches long

easy

dragonfly tails

Design by Jess Italia-Lincoln, courtesy of Vintaj Natural Brass Co.

Jess was inspired to make these earrings by summer days relaxing at the lake, watching dragonflies swirling past and showing off their beautiful iridescent colors shimmering in the sun.

INSTRUCTIONS

1) Trim one head pin to ½ inch long; string one dark amethyst seed bead. Form a small loop at top of wire leaving remaining wire exposed.

2) Trim another head pin to ¾ inch long; string one Caribbean blue crystal. Form a small loop at top of wire leaving remaining wire exposed.

3) String one opaque magenta seed bead and one metallic gold cube bead onto a 1-inch head pin. Form a small loop at top of wire leaving remaining wire exposed.

4) Form a loop with dragonfly's tail bringing it up behind wings.

5) Open a jump ring and slide on all three beaded dangles with longest dangle in the center. Attach ring to loop at bottom of dragonfly. Close ring.

6) Open loop on an ear wire and attach to top hole on dragonfly; close loop.

7) Repeat steps 1–6 for second earring, making sure dangles hang opposite of one another beside longest dangle.

Sources: Natural brass components (wholesale) from Vintaj Natural Brass Co.; all other beads and natural brass components (retail) from Galena Beads.

MATERIALS

- 2 (4mm) Caribbean blue opal AB2X CRYSTALLIZED™ - Swarovski Elements bicone crystals
- 2 (3mm) metallic gold iris miyuki cube beads
- 2 (11/0) opaque magenta Japanese seed beads
- 2 (8/0) transparent dark amethyst seed beads
- 2 (17 x 17mm) natural brass 2-hole dragonfly connectors
- 2 (5.25mm) natural brass jump rings
- 6 (1-inch) 21-gauge natural brass head pins
- 2 (20 x 15mm) natural brass round loop ear wires
- Round-nose pliers
- Chain-nose pliers
- Flush cutters

FINISHED SIZE

2 inches long

easy

lhasa drops

Design by Rupa Balachandar

Inspired by the beauty of traditional Tibetan jewelry, this pair of earrings uses the time-honored combination of turquoise, coral and sterling silver.

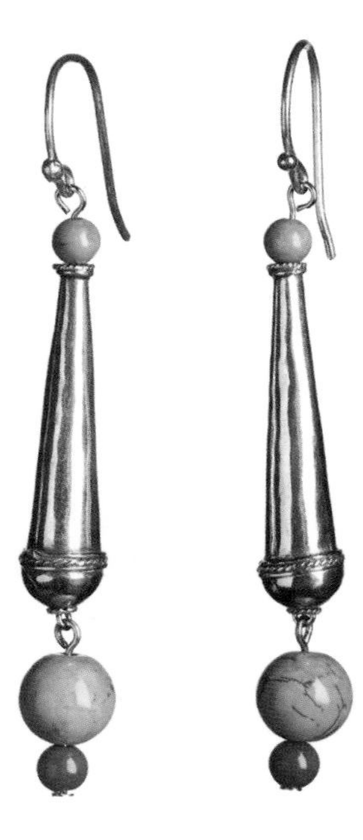

INSTRUCTIONS

1) Slide a coral bead and a 10mm turquoise bead on a head pin. Form a loop; trim excess wire.

2) Open loop and attach to loop on another eye pin; close loop. Slide a silver tubular bead onto eye pin along with a 4mm turquoise bead. Form a loop; trim excess wire.

3) Open loop and slide onto loop on ear wire; close loop.

4) Repeat steps 1–3 for second earring.

Source: Beads and ear wires from RupaB Designs.

MATERIALS

2 (10 x 35mm) sterling silver tubular beads

Reconstituted turquoise round beads: 2 (10mm), 2 (4mm)

2 (5mm) red coral round beads

2 (1-inch) silver head pins

2 (2½-inch) silver eye pins

2 sterling silver French ear wires

Round-nose pliers

Chain-nose pliers

Wire nippers

FINISHED SIZE

3 inches long

intermediate

tree of life

Design by Jess Italia-Lincoln, courtesy of Vintaj Natural Brass Co.

Reflecting early spring's many shades of green, new blooms and budding trees flourish their vibrant lush layers over last season's frost.

INSTRUCTIONS

1) Slide one green/brown rondelle, one 7.25mm closed jump ring (as a spacer) and one lime crystal onto a 1-inch head pin. Form a loop; trim excess wire.

2) Slide one pearl onto a 1½-inch head pin. Form a wrapped loop, attaching loop to a 5.25mm jump ring before wrapping. Trim excess wire.

3) Slide one molted rondelle onto a 1½-inch head pin. Form a wrapped loop, attaching loop to a 7.25mm jump ring before wrapping.

4) Slide one glass drop onto a 1-inch eye pin. Hold bead at center of eye pin. Bring both wire ends above bead; wrap straight wire end around wire just below loop, securing bead to wire. Open loop and attach to jump ring from step 3.

5) Attach jump ring from steps 3 and 4 to lower left or right side of tree of life pendant.

6) Attach jump ring from step 1 onto opposite side of pendant.

7) Attach a 5.25mm jump ring to a filigree drop; attach another 5.25mm jump ring to first 5.25mm jump ring. Open second jump ring and string it through both 7.25mm jump rings attached to pendant; close ring.

8) Open jump ring attached to pearl and string it through top loop of pendant; slide another 5.25mm jump ring onto first jump ring before closing. Open second jump ring and attach to loop on ear wire; close ring.

9) Repeat steps 1–8 for second earring, making sure beaded dangles are on opposite sides of pendant.

Sources: Natural brass components (wholesale only) from Vintaj Natural Brass Co.; all other beads and natural brass components (retail) from Galena Beads.

MATERIALS

2 (6mm) lime CRYSTALLIZED™ - Swarovski Elements bicone crystals
2 (4mm) olive potato pearls
Czech glass faceted rondelles: 2 (5 x 3mm) molted, 2 (8 x 6mm) green/brown
2 (9 x 6mm) olive/turquoise glass drops
2 (8 x 12mm) natural brass filigree teardrops
2 (20 x 24mm) natural brass tree of life pendants
Natural brass jump rings: 4 (7.25mm), 8 (5.25mm)
Natural brass head pins: 4 (1½-inch) 24-gauge, 2 (1-inch) 21-gauge
2 (1-inch) 21-gauge natural brass eye pins
2 (10 x 20mm) natural brass French ear wires
Round-nose pliers
Chain-nose pliers
Flush cutters

FINISHED SIZE

2¼ inches long

intermediate

peace pearls

Design by Barb Switzer

In mythology, the olive branch was considered the most useful gift given to humans by Athena, the Greek goddess of wisdom. It takes many years to grow a fruitful olive tree, but only a few minutes to make these classically simple earrings.

INSTRUCTIONS

1) Open loop on ear wire and slide on top loop of olive branch; close loop.

2) Slide a 6mm pearl on a head pin; form a wrapped loop, attaching loop to bottom of olive branch before wrapping. Trim excess wire. Repeat two more times with 3mm pearls, attaching them on each side of 6mm pearl.

3) Repeat steps 1 and 2 for second earring.

Source: All materials from Fusion Beads.

MATERIALS

Light green CRYSTALLIZED™ - Swarovski Elements crystal pearls: 4 (3mm), 2 (6mm)
6 (1-inch) sterling silver ball-tip head pins
2 (32.3 x 8.3mm) sterling silver olive branch links
2 sterling silver ear wires
Round-nose pliers
Chain-nose pliers
Wire nippers

FINISHED SIZE

2 inches long

intermediate

whispering leaves

Design by Brenda Morris Jarrett

Using an oak leaf paper punch on 36-gauge copper tooling foil will give you a shimmering whisper of leaves to dangle from your ears. They are so lightweight, that the slightest movement will send them "falling."

INSTRUCTIONS

1) Punch two leaves from tooling foil. Flatten each leaf gently with flat-nose pliers. Form a small loop at stem end of each leaf.

2) Form a wrapped loop at one end of a 2-inch length of 24-gauge wire. String a copper rondelle, green jasper heishi and a copper rondelle. Form a wrapped loop, attaching loop to small loop on a foil leaf before wrapping. Trim excess wire.

3) Use fine-tip pen to make a small dot 1 inch from end of a 3-inch 20-gauge wire. Form a small loop at end of wire nearest 1-inch mark; use flat-nose pliers to curl wire into a spiral up to 1-inch mark.

4) Place wire on steel block and flatten spiral with chasing hammer. Bend wire around a plastic pen to shape into an ear wire. Bend wire up at straight end with flat-nose pliers approximately ⅛ inch. Lightly tap ear wire with rubber mallet to harden.

5) Referring to photo, use flat-nose pliers to bend spiral to side.

6) Slide beaded dangle onto ear wire, sliding it up behind spiral. Flatten swirl slightly to catch dangle.

7) Repeat steps 2–6 for second earring, making this earring a mirror opposite of first earring. ●

Sources: Copper wire and rondelles from Fire Mountain Gems and Beads; green jasper heishi beads from Thunderbird Supply Co.; copper tooling foil from Hobby Lobby Stores Inc.; oak leaf punch from Martha Stewart Crafts.

MATERIALS

2 (6mm) green jasper stone heishi cylinder beads
4 (4mm) copper rondelles
Copper wire: 2 (2-inch) lengths 24-gauge, 2 (3-inch) lengths 20-gauge
2 x 2-inch 36-gauge copper metal tooling foil
Round-nose pliers
Flat-nose pliers
Needle-nose pliers
Wire nippers
Oak leaf punch
Chasing hammer
Rubber mallet
Steel bench block

FINISHED SIZE

2¼ inches long

easy

in the loop

Design by Laurie D'Ambrosio

Use circular links and jump rings to make a swinging fashion statement. This design will also work with shell rings, O rings and small doughnuts.

INSTRUCTIONS

1) Hold one eye pin up against reverse side of a turquoise ring with loop pointing upward. Bend wire below loop around ring, forming a large loop, securing eye pin to ring. Trim excess wire. Open loop on ear wire and attach to original eye-pin loop; close loop.

2) Open and attach seven jump rings onto turquoise ring; close rings.

3) Slide a bugle bead onto a head pin. Form a loop; trim excess wire. Repeat two more times.

4) Open loops on beaded head pins. Attach one to center jump ring; skip one jump ring on each side of center jump ring and attach remaining beaded head pins.

5) Repeat steps 1–4 for second earring. ●

Sources: Turquoise rings from Plaid Enterprises Inc.; bugle beads from Blue Moon Beads; findings from Hirschberg Schutz & Co. Inc.

MATERIALS

2 (29mm) turquoise rings
6 (5mm) turquoise bugle beads
14 (10mm) silver jump rings
6 (1-inch) silver head pins
2 (2-inch) silver eye pins
2 silver fishhook ear wires
Round-nose pliers
Chain-nose pliers
Wire nippers

FINISHED SIZE

2¼ inches long

intermediate

loopy tuesday

Design by Barb Switzer

Cindy Gimbrone's freeform glass loops have an organic appeal. Adding subtle pearls brings out the beautiful ivory shades, providing a natural complement for brass chain and findings.

INSTRUCTIONS

1) Slide a pearl onto a head pin. Form a wrapped loop, wrapping loop onto top of pearl. Trim excess wire.

2) Slide a pearl onto another head pin and form a wrapped loop in the same manner as before, attaching loop to previous loop before wrapping. Trim excess wire.

3) Repeat step 2 two more times. All four dangles are attached to each other, creating a cluster.

4) Open loop on ear wire and slide on first wrapped loop from step 1. Slide end link of one length of chain onto loop.

5) Thread chain through glass link and attach other end chain link to ear-wire loop. Close loop.

6) Repeat steps 1–5 for second earring.

Sources: Glass links from Cindy Gimbrone Beads; pearls and head pins from Fusion Beads; chain and ear wires from Fire Mountain Gems and Beads.

MATERIALS

8 (5mm) champagne freshwater pearls
2 silver and ivory glass links
8 (24-gauge) brass head pins
2 brass ear wires
2 (1½-inch) lengths brass-plated chain
Round-nose pliers
Chain-nose pliers
Flush cutters

FINISHED SIZE

1¾ inches long

easy

dots & stripes on display

Design by Alexa Westerfield

Yellow and black are the perfect colors to wear when you want to stand out in the crowd.

INSTRUCTIONS

1) Open a jump ring and slide on one polka-dot bead; close ring.

2) Slide a yellow seed bead, black-and-white striped bead and a yellow seed bead on an eye pin. Form a loop; trim excess wire.

3) Open bottom loop of eye pin and slide on jump ring from step 1. Close loop.

4) Open ear-wire loop and attach to top loop of beaded eye pin; close loop.

5) Repeat steps 1–4 for second earring.

Sources: Polka-dot beads from Creative Impressions in Clay; seed beads, jump rings and ear wires from Jo-Ann Stores Inc.

MATERIALS

2 yellow and black polka-dot ceramic round beads with shank
2 (11mm) black-and-white striped acrylic cylinder beads
4 (6/0) yellow seed beads
2 silver-plated eye pins
2 (10mm) silver jump rings
2 silver-plated ear wires
Round-nose pliers
Chain-nose pliers
Wire nippers

FINISHED SIZE

2¼ inches long

intermediate

polymer rectangle

Design by Laurie D'Ambrosio

Use polymer clay and a small cutter to make simple, super lightweight earring components. Paint highlights the great woven texture.

INSTRUCTIONS

1) Roll a quarter-size piece of clay between fingers until it is warm and pliable. Roll out clay flat on ceramic tile. Place texture sheet facedown on clay and run roller over clay.

2) Use cutter to cut two rectangles from textured clay. Remove extra clay from tile, leaving rectangles rolled flat.

3) Use finger to gently rub paint across clay rectangles. Use needle to pierce a hole through each rectangle ⅛ inch from top.

4) Follow manufacturer's instructions to bake clay rectangles. Let cool completely.

5) Form a loop at one end of each 2-inch wire. Open loops and insert them through holes on front of rectangles. Close loops.

6) String a triangle bead on each wire. Form a loop after each bead, positioning loops so they go in opposite direction from first loops. Trim excess wire.

7) Open top loops and attach to ear wires; close loops.

Sources: Triangle beads from Blue Moon Beads; texture sheet and rectangle cutter from Makin's Clay.

MATERIALS

2 (4mm) black triangle beads
2 gold ear wires
2 (2-inch) lengths 20-gauge permanently colored gold wire
Black polymer clay
Gold acrylic paint
Round-nose pliers
Wire nippers
Clay texture sheet
¾-inch rectangle clay cutter
Clay roller
Embroidery needle
Small ceramic tile

FINISHED SIZE

1¾ inches long

intermediate

recycle with style

Design by Liz Revit, courtesy of E.A. Revit Inc.

Don't discard those aluminum pull tabs! Go green by dressing them up with some fabulous beads. These lightweight earrings are as much fun to wear as they are to make.

INSTRUCTIONS

Option A

1) Using the hammer and awl, punch a hole through center top of both tabs. File any sharp edges with a metal file or emery board.

2) Place one tab facedown on one of the curves of wooden dapping block. Place wooden punch on top of tab; hammer gently until you obtain desired curve on tab. Repeat for second tab.

3) String the following onto a 6-inch piece of wire: two dark peach seed beads, copper bead and two dark peach seed beads. Center beads on wire; place beaded section of wire inside bottom opening of a pull tab. Wrap both wire ends around sides of pull tab. Trim ends on back.

4) String the following onto a 6-inch piece of wire: one dark peach seed bead, copper bead and one dark peach seed bead. Center beads on wire and attach to top opening of pull tab in the same manner as in step 3.

5) Open a 7mm jump ring; slide jump ring through hole at top of tab. Close ring. Open a 5mm jump ring and attach it to previous 7mm jump ring; slide one ear-wire loop onto jump ring before closing.

6) Repeat steps 3–5 for second earring.

MATERIALS

4 (5mm) copper round beads
12 (11/0) dark peach lined crystal AB Miyuki seed beads
2 aluminum pull tabs
Sterling silver jump rings: 2 (5mm), 2 (7mm)
2 sterling silver ear wires
4 (6-inch) pieces 24-gauge sterling silver dead-soft wire
Wire nippers
Ball peen hammer
Wooden dapping block with wooden punch
Awl
Metal file or emery board

FINISHED SIZE

1⅝ inches long

MATERIALS

CRYSTALLIZED™ - Swarovski Elements bicone crystals: 2 (6mm) smoked topaz, 2 (4mm) light azore

8 (10/0) turquoise lustre Czech seed beads

4 (11/0) dark peach lined crystal AB Miyuki seed beads

2 aluminum pull tabs

Sterling silver jump rings: 2 (5mm), 2 (7mm)

2 sterling silver ear wires

4 (6-inch) pieces 24-gauge sterling silver dead-soft wire

Wire nippers

Ball peen hammer

Wooden dapping block with wooden punch

Awl

Metal file or emery board

FINISHED SIZE

1⅝ inches long

INSTRUCTIONS

Option B

1) Repeat steps 1–6 of Option A substituting the following beads: turquoise seed bead, smoked topaz bicone and a turquoise seed bead for step 3; dark peach seed bead, turquoise seed bead, light azore bicone, turquoise seed bead and dark peach seed bead for step 4.

MATERIALS
2 (4–5mm) silver Bali-style beads
2 (6mm) crystal copper CRYSTALLIZED™ - Swarovski Elements rondelles
8 (10/0) turquoise lustre Czech seed beads
4 (11/0) dark peach lined crystal AB Miyuki seed beads
2 aluminum pull tabs
Sterling silver jump rings: 2 (5mm), 2 (7mm)
2 sterling silver ear wires
4 (6-inch) pieces 24-gauge sterling silver dead-soft wire
Wire nippers
Ball peen hammer
Wooden dapping block with wooden punch
Awl
Metal file or emery board

FINISHED SIZE
1⅝ inches long

INSTRUCTIONS

Option C

1) Repeat steps 1–6 of Option A substituting the following beads: dark peach seed bead, turquoise seed bead, Bali-style bead, turquoise seed bead and dark peach seed bead for step 3; turquoise seed bead, crystal copper rondelle and a turquoise seed bead for step 4. ●

Sources: Copper beads from Beaded Impressions Inc.; Miyuki seed beads from Caravan Beads Inc.; Bali-style beads and Czech seed beads from A. C. Moore Inc.; CRYSTALLIZED™ - Swarovski Elements crystals, ear wires, jump rings and sterling silver wire from Fusion Beads.

long dangles

Daring, formal or ready for fun, long earrings add a little drama. Great for those with long hair or anyone looking for maximum sparkle and swing. Get 20 different ideas for earrings from 2½ inches and beyond.

intermediate

tara shoulder dusters

Design by Fernando Dasilva, courtesy of Fernando Dasilva Jewelry

Cubic zirconia brightly pops with elegant black onyx and rich gold vermeil. This versatile flower chain design can be long or short.

INSTRUCTIONS

1) Open one jump ring and slide on two flower connectors; close ring. Continue to use jump rings to connect seven flower connectors together, creating a flower chain. Repeat to make another flower chain.

2) Slide a faceted round bead on a head pin; form a loop. Trim excess wire. Repeat for each faceted round bead.

3) String a briolette onto center of one 3-inch gold wire. Bend both wire ends up above top of briolette; wrap one wire around other wire, securing briolette. Form other wire into a small loop around bottom petal in flower chain. Trim excess wire. Repeat once.

4) Open loops on ear wires and slide on top ends of flower chains; close loops.

5) Open loops on black beaded dangles from step 2 and attach to side loops of flower chains, skipping side loops of fifth flower connectors from top.

6) Open loops on orange beaded dangles and attach to side loops of empty flower connectors.

Sources: Cubic-zircon beads and briolettes from Bijoux Collection; flower connectors, jump rings, lever-back ear wires, head pins and German-style wire from Beadalon.

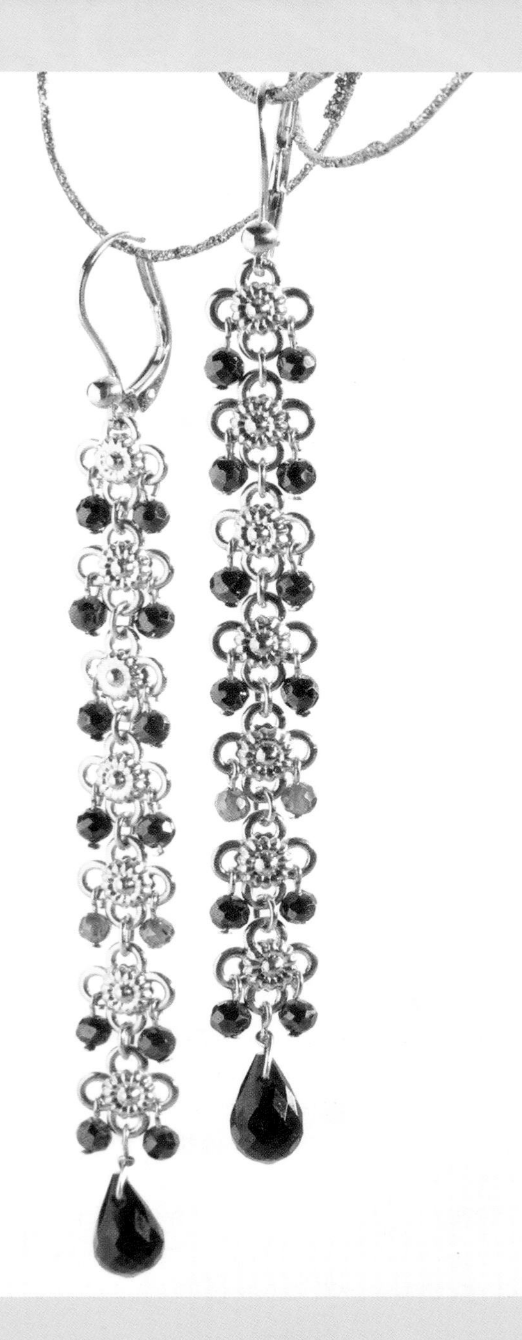

MATERIALS

3mm faceted cubic-zircon round beads: 24 black, 4 orange

2 black onyx faceted briolettes

14 gold-plated 4-way flower connectors

12 (4mm) gold-plated jump rings

28 (1-inch) gold-plated head pins

2 gold-plated lever-back ear wires with 3mm ball

2 (3-inch) lengths 24-gauge gold German-style wire

Round-nose pliers

Chain-nose pliers

Flush cutters

FINISHED SIZE

3½ inches long

easy

purple passion drops

Design by Alexa Westerfield

I love that these are sophisticated and glamorous all at the same time! The purple lucite jewels make a glitzy and playful statement!

Project note: *Use both pairs of chain-nose pliers to open jump rings.*

INSTRUCTIONS

1) Slide a pearl onto a head pin; form a loop. Trim excess wire. Repeat for each pearl.

2) Open one 15mm jump ring and slide on two more 15mm jump rings; close ring.

3) Open 8mm jump ring and attach to light purple faceted bead; slide jump ring onto one of the end jump rings from step 2. Close ring.

4) Open loop on a pearl head pin and attach it around both the first and second 15mm jump rings; close loop. Repeat to attach a second pearl head pin around second and third 15mm jump rings. Attach another pearl head pin to top 15mm jump ring.

5) Open loop on ear wire and attach to top 15mm jump ring and pearl head pin; close loop.

6) Repeat steps 2–5 for second earring.

Sources: Top-drilled beads from Hobby Lobby Stores Inc.; glass pearls from Wal-Mart Stores Inc.

MATERIALS

2 (22 x 18mm) lavender acrylic faceted top-drilled beads

6 (6mm) purple glass pearls

Silver jump rings: 6 (15mm), 2 (8mm)

6 silver-plated head pins

2 silver-plated ear wires

Round-nose pliers

2 pairs of chain-nose pliers

Wire nippers

FINISHED SIZE

3 inches long

intermediate

cleopatra

Design by Molly Schaller

Cleopatra makes a statement. Marquis-cut onyx hangs from gold-filled chain accented with iolite, onyx and labradorite stones.

INSTRUCTIONS

1) Cut chain into the following lengths: two 2-inch pieces and two 1-inch pieces. Cut wire into two 5-inch pieces.

2) String the following onto an eye pin: black onyx round, iolite rondelle, labradorite rondelle, iolite rondelle and black onyx round. Form a loop; trim excess wire.

3) Slide one black onyx round onto an eye pin. Form a loop and trim excess wire.

4) String a black onyx marquise onto center of a 5-inch wire. Bring both wire ends above center top of bead. Wrap one wire around other wire just above bead; form a small wrapped loop with other wire, attaching loop to center link of a 2-inch chain before wrapping. Trim excess wire.

5) Open one loop of beaded eye pin from step 2 and attach to end link of 2-inch chain with attached bead. Slide end link of one 1-inch chain onto loop before closing.

6) Open opposite loop of beaded eye pin and attach to opposite ends of 2-inch and 1-inch chains, making sure chains are not twisted.

7) Open one loop of beaded eye pin from step 3 and slide it onto center link of 1-inch chain; close loop. Open opposite loop and attach to loop of ear wire. Close loop.

8) Repeat steps 2–7 for second earring.

Sources: Beads, chain and wire from Fire Mountain Gems and Beads; eye pins and ear wires from Beadalon.

MATERIALS

6 (2mm) black onyx round beads
4 (3mm) iolite rondelles
2 (4mm) labradorite rondelles
2 (12 x 8mm) black onyx top-drilled marquise beads
4 (1-inch) gold eye pins
6 inches gold figure-8 chain
10 inches 26-gauge dead-soft gold-filled wire
2 gold ear wires
Round-nose pliers
Chain-nose pliers
Flush cutters

FINISHED SIZE

3¼ inches long

intermediate

warm bronze pearl chandeliers

Design by Sandy Parpart

Dream an evening of elegance to go with soft gold and glowing pearls. Classic chandelier findings meet their perfect match.

INSTRUCTIONS

1) Slide the following onto a head pin: bronze pearl and two silk crystals. Form a wrapped loop; trim excess wire. Attach a jump ring to wrapped loop and attach to top loop on chandelier component.

2) Slide the following onto a head pin: silk crystal, brown pearl, silk crystal, bronze pearl and a silk crystal. Form a wrapped loop; trim excess wire. Attach a jump ring to wrapped loop. Repeat two more times.

3) Open jump rings and attach to bottom loops on chandelier component; close loop.

4) Repeat steps 1–3 for second earring.

Sources: CRYSTALLIZED™ - Swarovski Elements crystal pearls and crystals from Fusion Beads; chandelier components and ear wires from Hirschberg Schutz & Co. Inc.

MATERIALS

CRYSTALLIZED™ - Swarovski Elements crystal pearls:
8 (6mm) bronze,
6 (5mm) brown

22 (4mm) silk CRYSTALLIZED™- Swarovski Elements bicone crystals

8 (1½-inch) gold-plated head pins

8 (5mm) gold-plated jump rings

2 (3-into-1) gold chandelier components

2 gold lever-back ear wires

Round-nose pliers

Needle-nose pliers

Wire nippers

FINISHED SIZE

3 inches long

easy

jet bicone dangles

Design by Sandy Parpart

Sleek formality is encapsulated by black bicone crystals and sterling silver. Stack them long for extra drama or shorter for versatility.

INSTRUCTIONS

1) Slide a bicone crystal onto a head pin; form a wrapped loop. Trim excess wire.

2) Open loop on an eye pin and attach to previous wrapped loop. String a bicone crystal. Form a wrapped loop; trim excess wire.

3) Repeat step 2 three more times.

4) Open loop on ear wire and attach to previous wrapped loop; close loop.

5) Repeat steps 1–4 for second earring.

Source: All materials available from Fusion Beads.

MATERIALS

10 (8mm) black CRYSTALLIZED™ - Swarovski Elements bicone crystals

2 (2-inch) 24-gauge sterling silver head pins

8 (2-inch) 24-gauge sterling silver eye pins

2 sterling silver fishhook ear wires

Round-nose pliers

Needle-nose pliers

Wire nippers

FINISHED SIZE

3 inches long

easy

loopy silver beads

Design by Carole Rodgers

These funky, loopy, wrapped silver wire beads make an unusual set of earrings. You may not be able to find it at first but each bead has a definite hole. Four beads and a few findings make a truly unique pair of earrings.

INSTRUCTIONS

1) String a silver round bead, loopy wire bead and a silver round bead on a head pin; form a wrapped loop. Trim excess wire. Repeat for each loopy wire bead.

2) Use jump rings to attach one end of 3-link chains to small loopy wire beaded head pins and one end of 9-link chains to large loopy wire beaded head pins.

3) Open a jump ring and slide on end links of two chains, one of each size; attach jump ring to loop on ear wire. Close jump ring. Repeat for second earring.

Sources: Loopy wire beads from Oriental Trading Co.; findings from Beadalon.

MATERIALS

Silver round loopy wire beads: 2 (20mm), 2 (12mm)
8 (3.5mm) silver round beads
4 (2-inch) silver ball-tip head pins
6 (4mm) silver jump rings
2 silver ear wires
Fine silver chain: 2 (3-link) pieces, 2 (9-link) pieces
Round-nose pliers
Chain-nose pliers
Flush cutters

FINISHED SIZE

2½ inches long

easy

dangle charm earrings

Design by Kristal Wick, courtesy of Sassy Silkies

Dragonflies dangle at the end of light, soft silk beads the color of the sky. Dream of flight, summer or anything these whimsical beauties inspire.

INSTRUCTIONS

1) Open loop on eye pin and slide on charm; close loop.

2) String beads as follows: bicone, pearl, scroll bead, pearl and bicone. Form a loop. Trim excess wire.

3) Open loop on ear wire and slide on beaded dangle; close loop.

4) Repeat steps 1–3 for second earring.

Sources: Sassy Silky beads from Sassy Silkies/Kristal Wick; CRYSTALLIZED™ - Swarovski Elements bicone crystals from Fusion Beads; charms and findings from Artbeads.com.

MATERIALS

2 Sassy Silky scroll beads
4 (4mm) Montana AB2X CRYSTALLIZED™ - Swarovski Elements bicone crystals
4 white freshwater pearls
2 silver dragonfly charms
2 silver eye pins
2 silver ear wires
Round-nose pliers
Flat-nose pliers
Wire nippers

FINISHED SIZE

3½ inches long

intermediate

blouse buttons

Design by Allison Hoffman, courtesy of Fusion Beads

Classic pearls inspired Allison to make these simple earrings. Sterling silver closed jump rings make the perfect frame for white crystal pearls.

Project note: *Use both pairs of chain-nose pliers to open jump rings.*

INSTRUCTIONS

1) String one pearl on a head pin; form a wrapped loop. Trim excess wire. Repeat for each pearl.

2) Open one 6mm jump ring and slide on one pearl dangle and two closed 18mm jump rings. Close ring.

3) Open one 6mm jump ring and slide on a pearl dangle and one of the 18mm jump rings from step 2. Close ring.

4) Open another 6mm jump ring and attach to 6mm jump ring from step 3 and loop on ear wire; close ring.

5) Repeat steps 2–4 for second earring.

Source: All materials from Fusion Beads.

MATERIALS

4 (8mm) white CRYSTALLIZED™ - Swarovski Elements crystal pearls

Sterling silver jump rings: 4 (18mm) heavy closed, 6 (6mm)

4 (1½-inch) 24-gauge sterling silver head pins

2 (15mm) sterling silver French ear hoops with 2mm bead

Round-nose pliers

2 pairs of chain-nose pliers

Flush cutters

FINISHED SIZE

2½ inches long

easy

marguerite

Design by Molly Schaller

Marguerite is sophisticated but not stuffy—fun without being too fluffy. Sterling silver links support mixed aqua crystals and blush pearls.

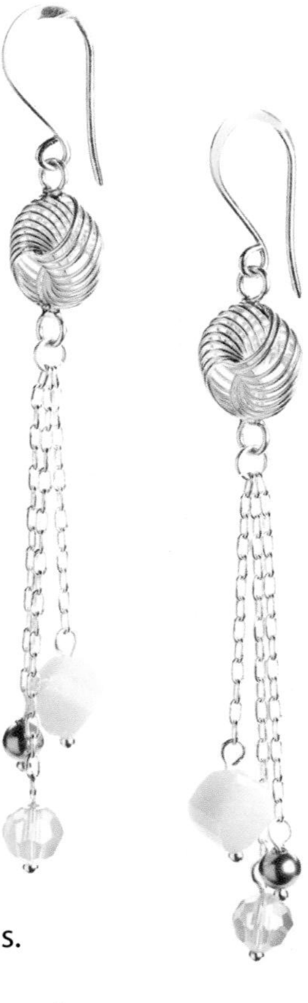

INSTRUCTIONS

1) Cut chain as follows: two 1-inch pieces, two 1¼-inch pieces and two 1½-inch pieces.

2) Slide one helix crystal onto a head pin; form a loop. Trim excess wire. Repeat for each crystal and pearl.

3) Open loops on beaded head pins. Attach helix crystals to 1-inch chains, pearls to 1¼-inch chains and round crystals to 1½-inch chains.

4) Open one jump ring; slide end links of three chains, one of each length, onto jump ring. Attach ring to a spiral link; close ring. Repeat once.

5) Open loops on ear wires and slide on opposite loops of spiral links; close loops. ●

Sources: Crystals and crystal pearls from CRYSTALLIZED™ - Swarovski Elements; swirl links and chain from Fire Mountain Gems and Beads; head pins and jump rings from Beadalon.

MATERIALS

2 (4mm) bronze CRYSTALLIZED™-Swarovski Elements crystal pearls

CRYSTALLIZED™-Swarovski Elements crystals: 2 (8mm) mint alabaster helix, 2 (6mm) pacific opal round

2 (17 x 10mm) sterling silver swirl links

6 silver ball-tip head pins

2 (4mm) silver jump rings

2 silver ear wires

8 inches sterling silver chain

Round-nose pliers

Chain-nose pliers

Flush cutters

FINISHED SIZE

3¼ inches long

intermediate

dancing stars

Design by Caito Amorose

Close your eyes, reach for the golden crescent, make a wish and fasten your dreams to a dazzling star!

INSTRUCTIONS

1) Cut two 5-inch pieces and four 3-inch pieces of wire.

2) Open a 3mm jump ring and slide on end link of one chain; insert chain through hole at top of 28mm star pendant; slide opposite end of chain onto jump ring. Close ring. Repeat once.

3) Attach a 6mm jump ring to each 20mm star pendant.

4) Form a wrapped loop at one end of a 3-inch wire. String 16 (3mm) bicone crystals. Form a wrapped loop, attaching loop to a 20mm star before wrapping. Bend wire gently to form a crescent shape. Trim excess wire.

5) Repeat step 4.

6) Form a wrapped loop at one end of 5-inch wire, attaching loop to a 20mm star before wrapping.

7) String three 5mm bicone crystals, one beaded crescent, seven 5mm bicone crystals, another beaded crescent and four 5mm bicone crystals. Form a wrapped loop, attaching loop to 28mm star before wrapping. Bend wire gently to form a crescent shape. Trim excess wire.

8) Open loop of an ear wire and attach dangle. Close loop.

9) Repeat steps 4–8 for second earring.

Source: All materials from Fire Mountain Gems and Beads.

MATERIALS

Crystal AB CRYSTALLIZED™-Swarovski Elements star pendants: 2 (28mm), 6 (20mm)

Golden shadow CRYSTALLIZED™-Swarovski Elements bicone crystals: 28 (5mm), 64 (3mm)

Gold-filled jump rings: 6 (6mm), 2 (3mm)

2 gold-filled ear wires

2 (½-inch) lengths small gold chain

22 inches 24-gauge gold-filled wire

Round-nose pliers

Chain-nose pliers

Wire nippers

FINISHED SIZE

3¾ inches long

intermediate

pastel charms

Design by Laura Stafford, courtesy of Tucson Mountain Jewelry

These stylish earrings will make you feel extra special. Perfect any time you need soft colors and a dash of bling.

INSTRUCTIONS

1) String the following onto a head pin: two pearls, garnet crystal, barrel bead, garnet crystal and two pearls. Form a wrapped loop; trim excess wire.

2) Open loop on ear wire and slide on beaded dangle; close loop.

3) Repeat steps 1 and 2 for second earring.

Sources: CRYSTALLIZED™ - Swarovski Elements crystal pearls from Brightlings Beads; barrel beads and ear wires from Jayahame Bali; head pins from Fusion Beads.

MATERIALS

8 (6mm) rose CRYSTALLIZED™-Swarovski Elements crystal pearls
4 (6mm) garnet crystals
2 (5 x 6mm) sterling silver Bali barrel beads
2 sterling silver Bali head pins
2 (24 x 11mm) sterling silver Bali ear wires
Round-nose pliers
Chain-nose pliers
Wire nippers

FINISHED SIZE

2⅝ inches long

daisies

Design by Liz Revit, courtesy of E.A. Revit Inc.

Put your wire skills to work as you create these flowering earrings. A green thumb is not required!

INSTRUCTIONS

1) Cut an 8-inch piece of 20-gauge wire. Slide an aqua disk to center of wire; bend one side of wire at a right angle (Fig. 1).

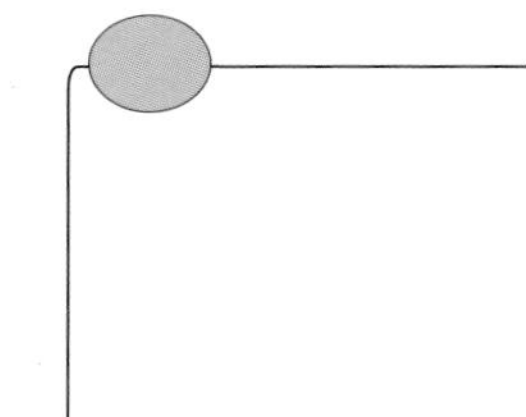

Fig. 1

2) Use round-nose pliers to form four petals with other side of wire, stringing a sterling silver bead on each petal as it is being formed. Wrap wire tail around wire on opposite side of bead (Fig. 2).

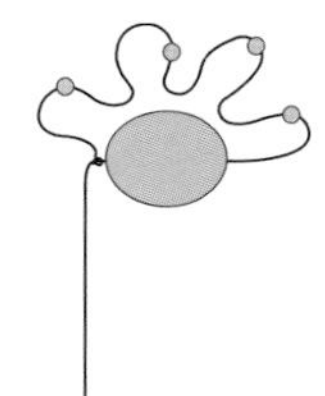

Fig. 2

3) Use chain-nose pliers to remove bend in wire from Fig. 1 and form wire into four petals as before (Fig. 3). Secure wire in the same manner as in step 2. Trim excess wire.

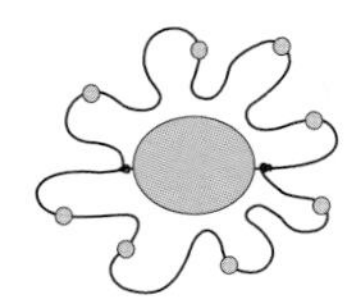

Fig. 3

4) Use hammer to gently tap petals on steel bench block, being careful not to hammer the beads. This will strengthen the metal.

5) Cut a 2-inch piece of 22-gauge wire. Form a wrapped loop at one end, attaching loop to one wire petal before wrapping. String a bronze bead. Form a wrapped loop, attaching loop to loop on ear wire before wrapping. Trim excess wire.

6) Repeat steps 1–5 for second earring. ●

Sources: Czech disk beads from Mode Beads; sterling silver beads, fire-polished beads, ear wires and wire from Fusion Beads.

MATERIALS

2 (10mm) aqua Czech disk beads
20 (2mm) sterling silver round beads
2 (4mm) bronze fire-polished oval beads
2 sterling silver ear wires
Sterling silver dead-soft wire: 16 inches 20-gauge, 4 inches 22-gauge
Round-nose pliers
Chain-nose pliers
Wire nippers
Ball peen hammer
Steel bench block

FINISHED SIZE

2¼ inches long

intermediate

when the shark bites

Design by Jean Yates

These art bead earrings balance the colors of pinkish bronze, blackish copper, jet, silver and gold. What more could you ask from such an unusual mix of metals and a dash of smoldering crystal?

INSTRUCTIONS

1) String the following onto a head pin: five heishi spacers, jet AB cube, five heishi spacers, shark bead, five heishi spacers, jet AB cube and five heishi spacers. Form a wrapped loop; trim excess wire. Repeat once, stringing the shark bead so shark faces opposite direction.

2) Use jump rings to attach beaded dangles to ear wires, using both pairs of chain-nose pliers to open jump rings.

Sources: Bottlecap beads from Glass Garden Beads; heishi spacers from Objects and Elements; CRYSTALLIZED™ - Swarovski Elements cubes from from Fusion Beads; snap-close jump rings from Via Murano.

MATERIALS

2 shark bottlecap beads
40 antique brass heishi spacers
4 (8mm) jet AB CRYSTALLIZED™ - Swarovski Elements cubes
2 (3-inch) 24-gauge gold-filled head pins
2 (6mm) gold-filled snap-close jump rings
2 gold-filled ear wires
Round-nose pliers
2 pairs of chain-nose pliers
Wire nippers

FINISHED SIZE

3 inches long

easy

swing it, sister

Design by Margot Potter

Sparkly, swingy earrings are sure to get attention, especially with your hair swept up in a 60s-style beehive. You can opt to make them shorter, but I'm a fan of big earrings. These would be positively perfect with a little A-line dress and some Grecian sandals.

Project note: *Use both pairs of chain-nose pliers to open jump rings.*

INSTRUCTIONS

1) Attach a jump ring to each briolette. Set aside.

2) Attach circles together as follows with jump rings: 12mm, 12mm and 25mm.

3) Slide first 12mm circle onto ear wire. Use pliers to gently squeeze ear wire around circle so it is stationary.

4) Slide a light rose briolette, erinite briolette and a light Colorado topaz briolette onto 25mm circle. Repeat three more times.

5) Repeat steps 2–4 for second earring. ***Note:*** *Slide briolettes on second earring in opposite direction so second earring is a mirror of first earring.*

6) Check back through to ensure jump rings are properly closed.

Sources: Briolettes from CRYSTALLIZED™ - Swarovski Elements; Quick Links and findings from Beadalon.

MATERIALS

CRYSTALLIZED™ - Swarovski Elements briolettes: 8 (12 x 6.5mm) erinite, 8 (11 x 5.5mm) light Colorado topaz, 8 (11 x 5.5mm) light rose

Open-center Quick Links circles: 4 (12mm), 2 (25mm)

28 (5mm) silver-plated jump rings

2 silver-plated large kidney ear wires

2 pairs of chain-nose pliers

FINISHED SIZE

3½ inches long

easy

waterfall clusters

Design by Carole Rodgers

These earrings use waterfall spacer bars as the foundation for hanging the tiny drop beads. They are a little time consuming to make but worth the effort.

Project note: *Use both pairs of chain-nose pliers to open jump rings.*

INSTRUCTIONS

1) Open a 4mm jump ring and place a drop bead on it; leave ring open. Repeat for remaining 71 drop beads. Set aside.

2) On one spacer bar, attach a bead jump ring to one end hole and the three middle holes, alternating sides of the bar. Repeat nine more times for a total of 10 single bars. Set aside.

3) On one spacer bar, attach a bead jump ring to each of the three middle holes, alternating sides of the bar. Repeat seven more times for a total of eight bars. Set aside.

4) Use a 3mm jump ring to attach end hole of one single bar to end hole of one bar from step 3.

5) Repeat step 4 three times for a total of four double bars.

6) Use a 3mm jump ring to attach one single bar to end hole of a double bar to create one triple bar.

7) Attach a bead jump ring to each 3mm jump ring used to attach spacer bars together.

8) Use a 3mm jump ring at the end of each bar to attach one single bar, one double bar, one triple bar, one double bar and one single bar to a closed 4mm jump ring.

9) Attach closed 4mm jump ring to another 4mm jump ring; attach second 4mm jump ring to a third 4mm jump ring. Attach last ring to ear wire.

10) Repeat steps 4–9 for second earring.

Source: Waves spacer bars, jump rings and ear wires from Beadalon.

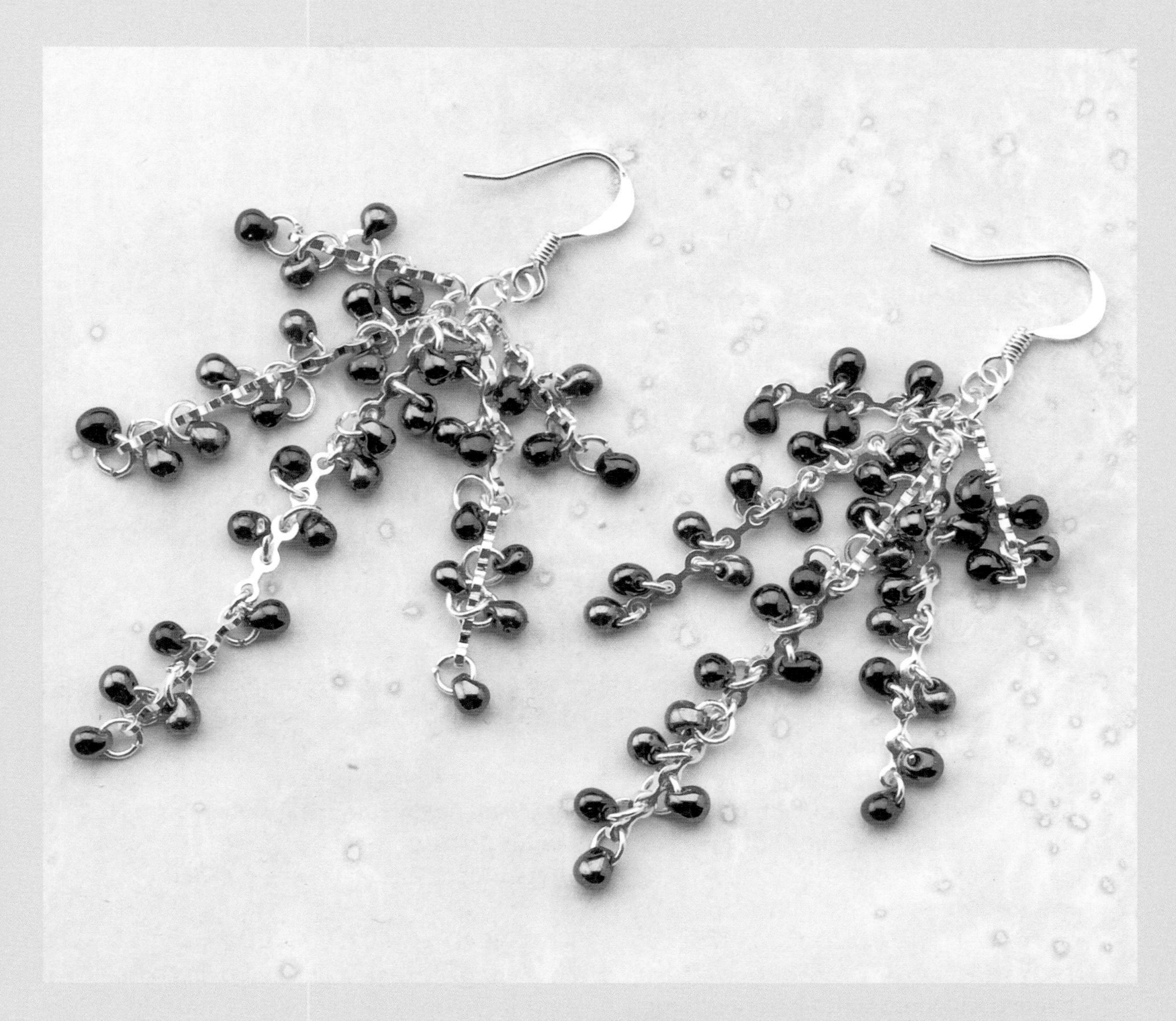

MATERIALS

72 purple AB drop beads
18 (5-hole) silver waves spacer bars
Silver jump rings: 78 (4mm), 18 (3mm)
2 silver ear wires
2 pairs of chain-nose pliers

FINISHED SIZE

3 inches long

intermediate

copper craze

Design by Laura McIvor

Copper and sterling are a classic and stunning combination. Learn to hammer wire to give it strength and texture, plus get some practice at spirals, a wire jewelry fundamental.

INSTRUCTIONS

1) Cut a 6-inch piece of 20-gauge sterling silver wire. Form a wrapped loop at one end. String the following: 4mm copper bead, daisy spacer, 8mm copper bead, daisy spacer and a 4mm copper bead. Form a wrapped loop; trim excess wire.

2) Cut a 5-inch piece of 18-gauge sterling silver wire. Form a spiral at one end, leaving a ½-inch tail. Form a small loop at end of ½-inch tail. Referring to photo, use chain-nose pliers to twist small loop 90 degrees.

3) Use small anvil and planishing hammer to flatten and harden the spiral. Hammer small loop to work harden wire and provide added strength.

4) Repeat steps 2 and 3 with copper wire.

5) Open a jump ring and slide on sterling silver and copper dangles; slide jump ring onto beaded wire from step 1 before closing.

6) Open loop on ear wire and attach to opposite end of beaded wire; close loop.

7) Repeat steps 1–6 for second earring.

Source: Copper beads from Capilano Rock & Gem.

MATERIALS

Wire: 12 inches 20-gauge sterling silver, 10 inches 18-gauge sterling silver, 10 inches 18-gauge copper

Copper round beads: 4 (4mm), 2 (8mm)

4 (5mm) silver daisy spacers

2 (5mm) 16-gauge silver jump rings

2 silver ear wires

Round-nose pliers

Chain-nose pliers

Wire nippers

Planishing hammer

Small anvil

FINISHED SIZE

2½ inches long

easy

chain cascade

Design by Allison Hoffman, courtesy of Fusion Beads

Earrings have never been so easy! Varying lengths of chain and jump rings combine to simulate cascading water in these stunningly simple earrings.

Project note: *Use both pairs of chain-nose pliers to open jump rings.*

INSTRUCTIONS

1) Cut silver chain as follows: two 3-inch lengths, four 2¼-inch lengths, two 2½-inch lengths and two 2¾-inch lengths.

2) Set aside one 3-inch length, two 2¼-inch lengths, one 2¾-inch length and one 2½-inch length for second earring.

3) Cut gunmetal chain into two 1½-inch lengths, making sure each length is made up of four large links connected by three small links.

4) Open a jump ring and slide on chains in the following order: one 1½-inch gunmetal, one 3-inch silver, one 2¼-inch silver, one 2½-inch silver, one 2¼-inch silver and one 2¾-inch silver. Close jump ring.

5) Open a second jump ring. Use this jump ring to connect jump ring with chains to loop on ear wire making sure gunmetal chain is facing outward; close ring.

6) Holding all lengths of silver chain, drape them through second large link of gunmetal chain, then through fourth large link of gunmetal chain creating a woven effect with chain.

7) Repeat steps 4–6 for second earring. ●

Source: All materials from Fusion Beads.

MATERIALS

Base metal chain: 25½ inches
- 2mm silver, 3½ inches
- 6mm gunmetal

4 (6mm) silver jump rings

2 silver lever-back ear wires

2 pairs of chain-nose pliers

Wire cutters

FINISHED SIZE

3¾ inches long

intermediate

spiral earrings

Design by Jennifer Heynen, courtesy of Jangles

There are all kinds of possibilities with this design. The spiral design is as playful and versatile as the ceramic bead at the bottom!

INSTRUCTIONS

1) Grab end of a 6-inch wire with needle-nose pliers and begin to form a spiral. Once wire has been turned around once, grab beginning of spiral with flat-nose pliers and continue to form a small spiral.

2) String a lime seed bead, silver disk, ceramic bead and a silver disk. String six lime seed beads, one black seed bead, six lime seed beads, one black seed bead and six lime seed beads.

3) Carefully wrap beaded wire around a pencil to form a spiral. Form a wrapped loop at end of wire; trim excess wire.

4) Open loop on ear wire and slide on beaded wire; close loop.

5) Repeat steps 1–4 for second earring.

Source: Ceramic beads, seed beads and silver disks from Jangles.

MATERIALS

- 2 zebra striped ceramic round beads
- 6/0 seed beads: 38 lime, 4 black
- 4 (6mm) silver disks
- 2 silver ear wires
- 2 (6-inch) lengths 20-gauge sterling silver wire
- Round-nose pliers
- Chain-nose pliers
- Wire nippers

FINISHED SIZE

3 inches long

intermediate

icy hot earrings

Design by Caito Amorose

Show your versatile personality wearing these three-dimensional chandelier sparklers. Icy facets of light shimmer and shine in a design that is hot hot hot!

INSTRUCTIONS

1) Cut two 2-inch pieces and four 1½-inch pieces of wire.

2) Form a wrapped loop at one end of one 1½-inch wire. String the following: bicone, rondelle and a dice bead. Form another wrapped loop. Trim excess wire. The dice end will be the top of the beaded link. Repeat once.

3) String the following onto a head pin: bicone, rondelle, dice bead, bicone, two rondelles, bicone, dice bead, bicone, two rondelles and a bicone. Form a wrapped loop, attaching loop to bottom of one beaded link from step 2 before wrapping. Trim excess wire.

4) String the following onto a head pin: bicone, rondelle, dice bead, bicone, dice bead, bicone and a dice bead. Form a wrapped loop. Trim excess wire. Repeat once.

5) Form a wrapped loop at one end of a 2-inch wire, attaching loop to a beaded dangle from step 4 before wrapping. Trim excess wire.

6) String a bicone, rondelle and a dice bead onto wire from step 5. Insert wire through top loops of beaded links from step 2. String a dice bead, rondelle and a bicone. Form a wrapped loop, attaching loop to remaining beaded dangle from step 4 before wrapping. Trim excess wire.

7) Open loop on ear wire and slide on empty wrapped loop on beaded link. Close loop.

8) Repeat steps 2–7 for second earring.

Source: All materials from Fire Mountain Gems and Beads.

MATERIALS

24 (6mm) crystal clear CRYSTALLIZED™-Swarovski Elements dice beads

30 (3mm) crystal AB CRYSTALLIZED™-Swarovski Elements bicone crystals

22 (6mm) quartz crystal flat rondelles

6 (2-inch) sterling silver head pins

2 sterling silver ear wires

10 inches 24-gauge sterling silver wire

Round-nose pliers

Chain-nose pliers

Wire nippers

FINISHED SIZE

3½ inches long

intermediate

ombre leaves

Design by Heather Powers

These earrings are a quick and easy way to jazz up some craft store findings. Using a simple color mixing technique with polymer clay you can create beautiful color gradations. This technique is known as the Skinner Blend.

Project note: *Follow manufacturer's instructions for clay safety. Once a pan is used for clay, it should not be used for cooking food.*

INSTRUCTIONS

1) Cut off ¼ of a block of both colors of clay. Condition both pieces by kneading them with hands until they are warm and pliable. Set pasta machine to thickest setting and roll each piece of clay through machine into a rectangle.

2) Trim rectangles to approximately the same size and cut both in half diagonally to form two long triangles of each color.

3) Stack fuchsia triangles tip to tip, so that triangle is twice as thick. Repeat with turquoise triangles.

4) Place triangles next to each other to form a rectangle. Layer the two triangles slightly on top of each other so they stick together. Run clay rectangle vertically through pasta machine on thickest setting.

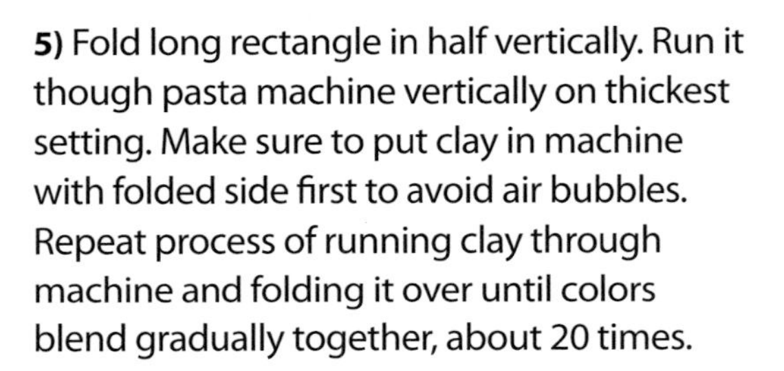

5) Fold long rectangle in half vertically. Run it though pasta machine vertically on thickest setting. Make sure to put clay in machine with folded side first to avoid air bubbles. Repeat process of running clay through machine and folding it over until colors blend gradually together, about 20 times.

6) Lay blended clay on top of card stock. Place leaf connector on top of clay and press down firmly. Cut around connector through clay with cutting blade; trim excess clay from sides and back. The clay should only be inside the metalwork. Repeat with other leaf connector. Bake according to manufacturer's directions.

7) Slide a silver seed bead and a purple glass bead onto a head pin; form a loop. Trim excess wire. Do not discard trimmed wire. Open loop and attach to bottom of leaf connector; close loop.

continued on page 169

MATERIALS

Polymer clay: fuchsia, turquoise
2 (4mm) fuchsia CRYSTALLIZED™-Swarovski Elements bicone crystals
2 (6mm) purple faceted glass round beads
2 silver seed beads
2 silver leaf connectors/links
2 (2-inch) silver head pins
2 silver ear wires
Card stock
Clay cutting blade
Round-nose pliers
Wire nippers
Pasta machine

FINISHED SIZE

2¼–2½ inches long

sets

Satisfy your need for more jewelry with necklaces and bracelets matched with even more earrings. Thirteen sets range from earthy and elegant to seasonal and bright to satisfy any mood.

easy

red hot glass set

Designs by Annie Destito, courtesy of Glass Bead Store

I was inspired to use these handmade glass beads in a bold and dramatic yet very traditional fashion. Each bead is handmade and unique adding variety and flare to this design.

INSTRUCTIONS

Earrings

1) String a seed bead, E bead, fire-polished bead, E bead and a seed bead on a head pin. Form a wrapped loop, forming wire tail into a small spiral pushing it against top beads. Repeat once.

2) Open loops on ear wires and slide on beaded head pins; close loops.

MATERIALS

10 glass bubble beads
14 (8mm) light red AB Czech glass fire-polished round beads
36 (8mm) purple freshwater pearls
6/0 metallic rainbow bronze glass seed beads
70 E beads in coordinating color
12 (2mm) silver-plated crimp beads
4 silver-plated split rings
2 sterling silver head pins
2 sterling silver ear wires
2 (10mm) silver-plated lobster-claw clasps
3–4mm silver-plated chain: 1 (2-inch) length, 1 (1¾-inch) length
34½ inches .018-inch-diameter 7-strand nylon-coated flexible beading wire
Round-nose pliers
Chain-nose pliers
Crimp pliers
Wire nippers
Tape

FINISHED SIZES

Earrings
1½ inches long

Necklace
19¼ inches (including clasp), plus a 3-inch extender chain

Bracelet
8 inches (including clasp), plus a 1¾-inch extender chain

Necklace

1) Cut a 20-inch length of wire. String seven bubble beads centered on wire, stringing a fire-polished bead before and after each bubble bead. ***Note:*** *String enough seed beads inside each bubble bead to fill holes.*

2) On each side of strand, string an alternating pattern of 14 E beads and 14 freshwater pearls, beginning with an E bead.

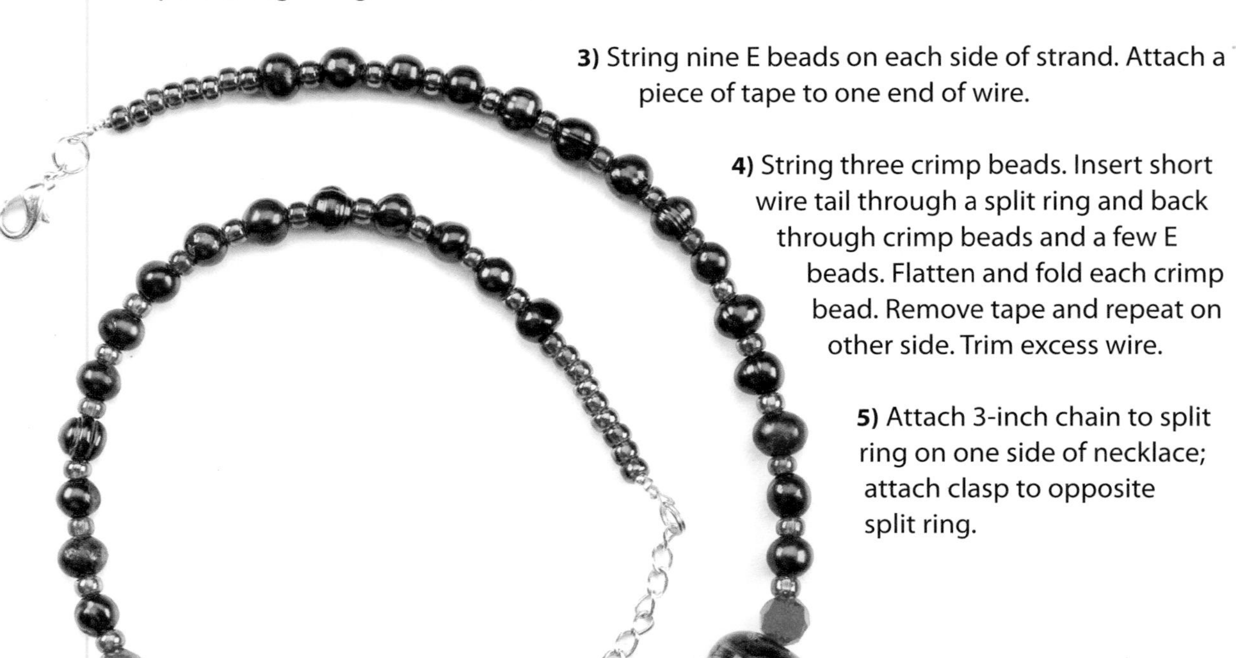

3) String nine E beads on each side of strand. Attach a piece of tape to one end of wire.

4) String three crimp beads. Insert short wire tail through a split ring and back through crimp beads and a few E beads. Flatten and fold each crimp bead. Remove tape and repeat on other side. Trim excess wire.

5) Attach 3-inch chain to split ring on one side of necklace; attach clasp to opposite split ring.

Bracelet

1) String three bubble beads centered on remaining 14½-inch wire, stringing a fire-polished bead before and after each bubble bead. ***Note:*** *String enough seed beads inside each bubble bead to fill holes.*

2) On each side of strand, string an alternating pattern of three to four freshwater pearls and three to four E beads, beginning with an E bead.

3) String five to six E beads on each side of strand. Attach a piece of tape to one end of wire.

4) Repeat steps 4 and 5 of Necklace, using 1¾-inch chain instead of 3-inch. ●

Sources: Glass bubble beads from Glass Bead Store; Czech glass beads and seed beads from Fire Mountain Gems and Beads.

intermediate

a little twisted

Designs by Laura McIvor

With a bit of wire, some interesting beads and a "twisted" sense of humor, this sterling charmer can be created in no time! Hand-wrapped sterling spirals add design interest to the piece.

INSTRUCTIONS

Earrings

1) Cut a 6-inch piece of 20-gauge wire. Form a wrapped loop at one end. String a rectangle bead. Form another wrapped loop. Wrap wire end around tip of round-nose pliers to form a small loop; use fingers to manipulate wire into a small spiral as shown.

2) Position spiral so it is perpendicular to rectangle bead. Place spiral on edge of anvil and hit it with planishing hammer to give it a flat finish.

3) Use fingers to press spiral flat against face of bead. The heat from your fingers will help to manipulate wire until it fits flush.

4) String a round bead on a head pin; form a wrapped loop, attaching loop to spiral loop on rectangle bead before wrapping. In the same manner as before, form wire end into a spiral.

5) Open loop on ear wire and slide on original wrapped loop; close loop.

6) Repeat steps 1–5 for second earring, stringing round bead first for a topsy-turvy effect if desired.

Bracelet

1) Cut a 6-inch piece of 20-gauge wire. Form a wrapped loop at one end. String a pillow bead. Refer to steps 1–3 for Earrings to form a spiral on bead.

2) Repeat step 1 four more times for a total of three rectangle links and two round links.

3) Attach a jump ring to both ends of each link from step 2.

4) Use one jump ring to connect a rectangle and round link together. There should be three jump rings between links. Repeat to connect all links together, alternating round and rectangle links.

continued on page 169

MATERIALS

Silver pillow beads: 6 round, 8 rectangle

7 (3-inch) silver ball-tip head pins

14 (4mm) 16-gauge silver jump rings

2 silver ear wires

Silver toggle clasp

42 inches silver 20-gauge wire

Round-nose pliers

Chain-nose pliers

Wire nippers

Planishing hammer

Small anvil

FINISHED SIZES

Earrings

2¼ inches long

Bracelet

7¾ inches (including clasp)

intermediate

mismatched mischief

Designs by Melissa Lee

These pieces were inspired by my young son who is himself a bit of a scamp. I created the word charms with him in mind and felt that Sarah Moran's cheerful and bright lampwork beads would complement the child-like theme perfectly.

INSTRUCTIONS

Earrings

1) Remove jump ring from "imp" charm. Open loop of one eye pin and attach to charm; close loop.

2) String a fuchsia satin crystal, lampwork bead and a 7mm pearl. Form a wrapped loop; trim excess wire.

3) Open a jump ring and slide on beaded eye pin; attach ring to loop on ear wire. Close jump ring.

4) Repeat steps 1–3 for second earring substituting "wag" charm for "imp" charm and an aquamarine crystal for fuchsia satin crystal.

Bracelet

1) String a crimp tube ½ inch from one end of beading wire; insert short wire tail through round end of clasp and back through crimp tube. Use crimp pliers to flatten the crimp tube.

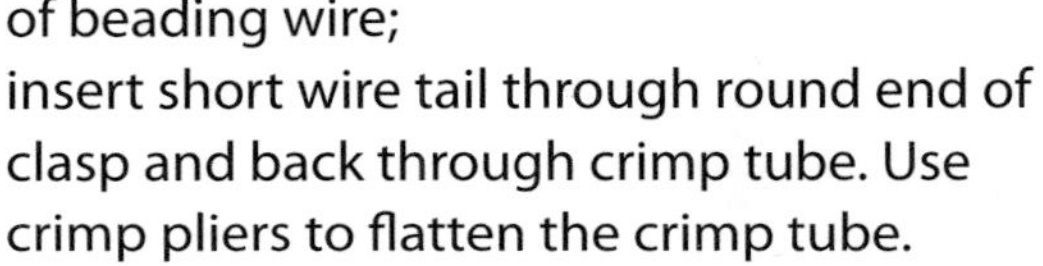

2) String one aquamarine crystal, "scamp" charm, two aquamarine crystals, three lampwork beads and 13 (9mm) pearls.

3) String a crimp tube. Insert wire through bar end of clasp and back through crimp tube and a few pearls. Flatten the crimp tube. Trim excess wire.

Sources: Mischief charms from Melissa J. Lee; lampwork beads from Sarah Moran; pearls, crimp tubes, eye pins and jump rings from Fire Mountain Gems and Beads; CRYSTALLIZED™ - Swarovski Elements crystals and toggle clasp from Turtle Island Beads; ear wires and beading wire from Chelsea's Beads.

MATERIALS

Fine silver and resin Mischief charms: 19mm blue “scamp,” 16mm pink “imp,” 16mm lavender “wag”
5 (17mm) ColorBlast Asterisk Tab lampwork beads in a variety of colors
White freshwater pearls: 13 (9mm), 2 (7mm)
CRYSTALLIZED™-Swarovski Elements round crystals: 4 (8mm) aquamarine, 1 (8mm) fuchsia satin
2 (2-inch) sterling silver eye pins
2 sterling silver micro crimp tubes
2 (5mm) sterling silver jump rings
2 sterling silver fishhook ear wires
Sterling silver toggle clasp
10 inches .010-inch-diameter nylon-coated flexible beading wire
Round-nose pliers
Chain-nose pliers
Crimp pliers
Wire nippers

FINISHED SIZES

Earrings

2¾ inches long

Bracelet

8 inches (including clasp)

easy

crystal clear

Designs by Suzann Wilson

This twisted triple-strand necklace and crystal earrings will turn heads at any event!

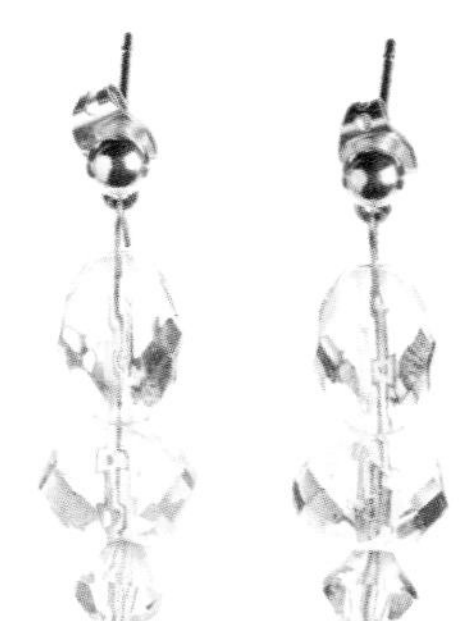

INSTRUCTIONS

Earrings

1) Slide the following on a head pin: clear AB bicone crystal, crystal AB rondelle and a crystal AB oval.

2) Form a loop; trim excess wire. Open loop and attach to ball post. Close loop.

3) Repeat steps 1 and 2 for second earring.

Necklace

1) String a crimp tube 1 inch from one end of a 20-inch piece of wire. Insert short wire tail through top hole on one half of clasp and back through crimp tube. Use crimp pliers to flatten and fold the crimp tube.

2) Repeat step 1 to attach second and third wire lengths to remaining two holes on clasp.

3) Randomly string 18 inches of crystals and one crimp tube on each strand.

4) Insert wire tail of one strand through top hole on other half of clasp and back through crimp tube, leaving ¼ inch of wire between crimp tube and last crystal. ***Note:*** *The ¼ inch allows strand to be properly twisted when necklace is complete.* Flatten and fold the crimp tube. Trim excess wire.

5) Repeat step 4 to attach remaining two wires to clasp.

6) Holding one end of necklace, twist necklace to desired tightness. Close clasp.

Sources: Crystals from CRYSTALLIZED™ - Swarovski Elements; glass beads from Michaels Stores Inc.; crimp tubes and beading wire from Beadalon; ball posts and head pins from Darice Inc.; slide-lock clasp from Fire Mountain Gems and Beads.

MATERIALS

6mm CRYSTALLIZED™ - Swarovski Elements bicone crystals: 12 clear, 2 clear AB

Clear CRYSTALLIZED™ - Swarovski Elements round crystals: 21 (10mm), 17 (12mm)

Crystal AB faceted glass beads: 20 (9 x 6mm) oval, 20 (8 x 4mm) rondelle

Crystal glass beads: 9 (8mm) beveled coin, 12 (9 x 11mm) oval, 23 (10mm) cross-cut

6 (2 x 2mm) sterling silver crimp tubes

2 sterling silver head pins

2 sterling silver ball posts

Sterling silver 3-strand slide-lock clasp

3 (20-inch) lengths .015-inch-diameter 49-strand nylon-coated flexible beading wire

Round-nose pliers

Crimp pliers

Wire nippers

FINISHED SIZES

Earrings

1¼ inches long

Necklace

16 inches when twisted (including clasp)

intermediate

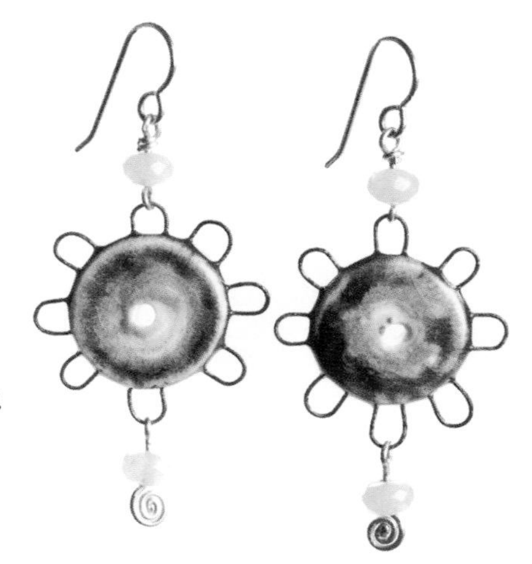

flower lula

Designs by Jennifer Heynen, courtesy of Jangles

Playful ceramic pinwheels are linked by soft blue apatite beads. Make this flower chain for everyday wear.

INSTRUCTIONS

Earrings

1) Grab end of a 2-inch wire with needle-nose pliers and turn wire once to begin a spiral; continue to form spiral using flat-nose pliers. String an apatite stone. Form a loop above stone, attaching loop to a 1-inch pinwheel bead before closing; trim excess wire.

2) Form a small loop at end of a 2-inch wire, attaching loop to opposite side of pinwheel bead before closing. String an apatite stone. Form a wrapped loop, attaching loop to loop on ear wire before wrapping. Trim excess wire.

3) Repeat steps 1 and 2 for second earring.

Bracelet

1) Form a wrapped loop at one end of a 2-inch wire, attaching loop to clasp before wrapping. String an apatite stone. Form another wrapped loop; trim excess wire.

2) Form a wrapped loop at one end of a 2-inch wire, attaching loop to previous wrapped loop before wrapping. String an apatite stone. Form another wrapped loop, attaching loop to a 1-inch pinwheel bead before wrapping. Trim excess wire.

3) In the same manner as in step 2, form another apatite link, connecting 1-inch pinwheel to 2-inch pinwheel. Repeat to attach another 1-inch pinwheel to opposite side of 2-inch pinwheel.

4) Make and connect two more apatite links to opposite side of 1-inch pinwheel in the same manner as in step 1, making last wire loop a little larger to accommodate clasp.

Sources: Ceramic pinwheel beads from Jangles; apatite stones from Dakota Stones.

MATERIALS

Red ceramic pinwheel beads: 4 (1-inch), 1 (1½-inch)

10 (6 x 8mm) apatite faceted stones

2 silver ear wires

Silver lobster-claw clasp

10 (2-inch) lengths 20-gauge sterling silver wire

Round-nose pliers

Chain-nose pliers

Wire nippers

FINISHED SIZES

Earrings

2½ inches long

Bracelet

7 inches (including clasp)

intermediate

sweet comic valentine

Designs by Fernando Dasilva, courtesy of Fernando Dasilva Jewelry

This design is a tribute to Rodgers and Hart, two American songwriters who wrote the timeless lyrics of "My Funny Valentine." The set is very delicate and its passion is represented by the purity of love reflected on the sparkly hearts. The earrings' heart links hang upside down because love sometimes turns you upside down.

INSTRUCTIONS

Heart Links

1) Make a cut through top center curved portion of one heart link, creating an opening. Dab a small amount of glue on end of link and insert into holes of one crystal heart. Repeat for each crystal heart for a total of five heart links. Set aside to dry.

Earrings

1) Slide an 8mm pearl, bead bumper and a siam AB crystal onto an eye pin. Form a loop; trim excess wire.

2) Open loop on pearl side of beaded eye pin and attach to a heart link; close loop. Open opposite loop and attach to loop on ear wire; close loop.

3) Repeat steps 1 and 2 for second earring.

MATERIALS

5 (14mm) crystal AB CRYSTALLIZED™ - Swarovski Elements crystal hearts
11 (6mm) siam AB CRYSTALLIZED™ - Swarovski Elements round crystals
Maroon CRYSTALLIZED™ - Swarovski Elements crystal pearls: 6 (6mm), 2 (8mm)
2 (2mm) clear cube Bead Bumpers
3 (6mm) silver-plated jump rings
15 (2-inch) silver-plated head pins
2 (2-inch) silver-plated eye pins
2 silver-plated lever-back ear wires
9 x 14mm silver-plated round magnetic clasp
5 (20 x 22.5mm) silver-plated heart Diamond Cut Quick Links
10 medium silver-plated Quick Link connectors
16 inches silver-plated round Quick Link chain
Round-nose pliers
Chain-nose pliers
Flush cutters
Bead adhesive

FINISHED SIZES

Earrings
2⅜ inches long

Necklace
19½ inches (including clasp)

Necklace

1) Slide a 6mm pearl onto a head pin; form a wrapped loop. Trim excess wire. Repeat five more times for a total of six pearl dangles.

2) In the same manner as in step 1, make nine siam AB dangles.

3) Using chain-nose pliers, attach one connector to both sides of the remaining three heart links.

4) Cut two round links from chain and attach to both sides of one heart link from step 3. Attach a heart link on each side of round links. This will be center portion of necklace.

5) Cut remaining chain into two 7-inch lengths. Attach lengths to each side of center portion.

6) Use connectors to attach one half of clasp to each end of necklace.

7) Open a jump ring and slide on two pearl dangles and three siam AB dangles. Repeat two more times. Attach rings to center heart link and round links next to center heart link. Close rings. ●

Sources: Crystals and crystal pearls from CRYSTALLIZED™ - Swarovski Elements; Quick Links components, Bead Bumpers, magnetic clasp, jump rings, eye pins, head pins and bead adhesive from Beadalon.

intermediate

sand & sky

Designs by Ishita Ghosh

Beautiful lampwork glass beads, reflecting the shades of sand and sky, combine with gemstones and metals for an earthy, casual elegance.

Project note: *Use both pairs of chain-nose pliers to open jump rings.*

INSTRUCTIONS

Earrings

1) String the following on a head pin: mystic black pearl, yellow jasper coin, 18 x 16mm Earthy Aqua lampwork bead and a yellow jasper round. Form a wrapped loop; trim excess wire. Repeat once.

2) Open loops on ear wires and slide on beaded head pins. Close loops.

Bracelet

1) Slide an 8mm black onyx round and a yellow jasper coin onto an eye pin. Form a wrapped loop; trim excess wire.

2) Slide a flat oval lava rock bead and an African yellow saucer onto an eye pin. Form a wrapped loop; trim excess wire.

3) Open loop on beaded eye pin from step 1 and attach to

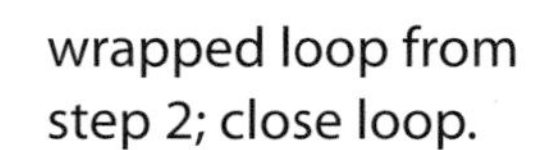

wrapped loop from step 2; close loop.

4) Open 6mm jump ring and slide on opposite end of beaded eye pin from step 2 along with another empty eye pin. Close ring.

5) Slide the 27 x 20mm lampwork bead onto eye pin. Form a wrapped loop; trim excess wire.

6) Open loop on another eye pin and attach to previous wrapped loop; close loop. String yellow jasper horse eye bead. Form a wrapped loop; trim excess wire.

7) Open loop of another eye pin and attach to previous wrapped loop; close loop. Slide the following onto eye pin: 4mm black onyx round, four African yellow saucers and turquoise rondelle. Form a wrapped loop. Trim excess wire.

8) Open one 8mm jump ring; slide on previous wrapped loop and ring attached to S clasp. Close ring.

continued on page 169

MATERIALS

5 (8mm) African yellow stone saucers
8mm turquoise faceted rondelle
Black onyx round beads: 1 (4mm), 1 (8mm)
25 x 18mm lava rock flat oval
Yellow jasper beads: 1 (28 x 15mm) horse eye, 3 (12mm) coin, 2 (4mm) round
Earthy aqua lampwork glass beads: 1 (27 x 20mm), 2 (18 x 16mm)
2 (11 x 8mm) mystic black CRYSTALLIZED™ - Swarovski Elements pear-shaped crystal pearls
13.5mm brass hammered soldered ring
Brass jump rings: 2 (8mm), 1 (6mm)
5 (2½-inch) brass eye pins
2 (3-inch) brass head pins
23 x 10mm brass S clasp with ring
2 brass ear wires
Round-nose pliers
2 pairs chain-nose pliers
Wire nippers

FINISHED SIZES

Earrings
2½ inches long

Bracelet
8¾ inches (including clasp)

intermediate

architectural elegance

Designs by Molly Schaller

Keystone crystals create sensuous curves in spring colors punctuated by chain and lustrous seed beads.

INSTRUCTIONS

Pendant

1) Grasp center of one 3-inch wire with round-nose pliers and bring wire ends around round nose to form a loop in center of wire. Slide one crystal teardrop onto loop. Form a small loop at each end of wire (Fig. 1).

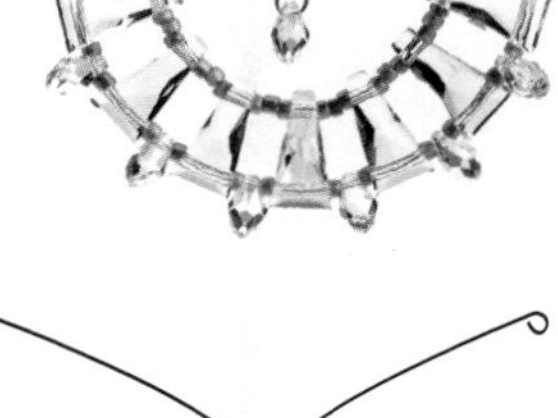
Fig. 1

2) Open small loops and slide on end links of one 3-inch chain; close loops.

3) Holding the two 24-inch lengths of beading wire together as one, string a crimp tube ½ inch from one end. Insert short wire tails through one of the small loops from step 2, making sure attached chain is in upper portion of loop. Pass wires back through crimp tube. Use crimp pliers to flatten and fold the crimp tube.

4) With wires still together, string one Pacific opal rondelle.

5) Separate wires. On top wire, string the following: three seed beads, top hole of one jonquil keystone bead, three seed beads, top hole of one peridot keystone bead, three seed beads, top hole of one aquamarine keystone bead, three seed beads, top hole of one AB crystal keystone bead, three seed beads, top hole of one aquamarine keystone bead, three seed beads, top hole of one peridot keystone bead, three seed beads, top hole of one jonquil keystone bead, three seed beads and one Pacific opal rondelle. Attach a bead stopper or tape to wire end.

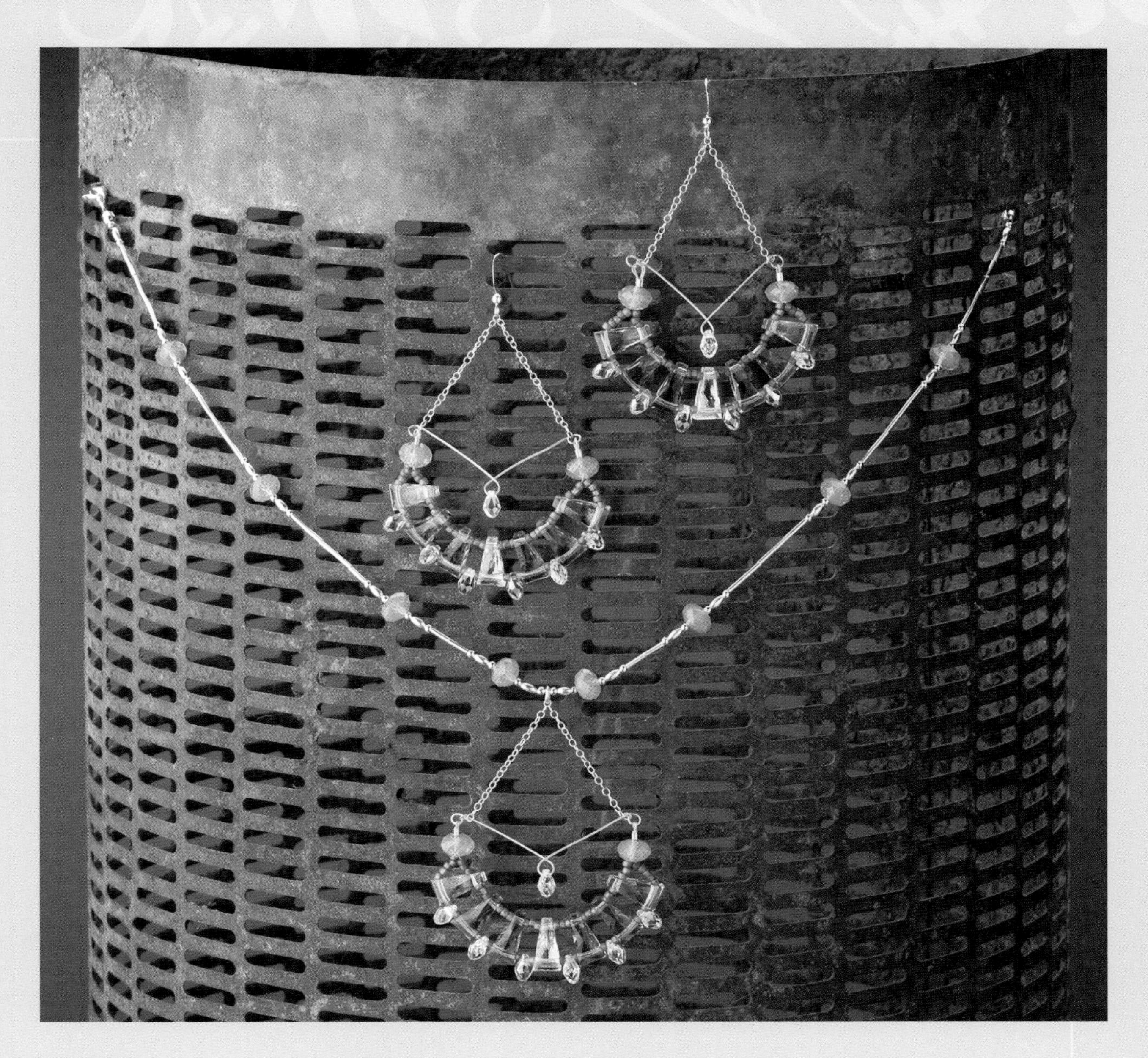

MATERIALS

13 x 7mm CRYSTALLIZED™ - Swarovski Elements keystone beads: 6 jonquil, 6 peridot, 6 aquamarine, 3 crystal AB
21 (7 x 4mm) crystal AB CRYSTALLIZED™ - Swarovski Elements teardrop pendants
14 (8mm) Pacific opal CRYSTALLIZED™ - Swarovski Elements rondelles
Silver beads:
 36 (2mm) round,
 18 (4mm) oval
34 (5mm) liquid silver tubes
138 sea blue seed beads
6 (1.3mm) silver crimp tubes
Silver jump rings: 1 (4mm), 1 (6mm)
2 silver Wire Guardians
2 Scrimp findings
2 sterling silver ear wires
Small silver lobster-claw clasp
3 (3-inch) lengths silver light cable chain
3 (3-inch) lengths 24 gauge sterling silver half-hard wire
.018-inch-diameter 49-strand silver-plated nylon-coated flexible beading wire:
 2 (24-inch) lengths,
 1 (20-inch) length
Bead stopper or tape
Round-nose pliers
Chain-nose pliers
Crimp pliers
Scrimp kit
Flush cutters
Wire nippers

FINISHED SIZES

Earrings
3½ inches long

Necklace
15 inches (including clasp), plus a 3-inch drop

6) String the following onto bottom wire: five seed beads, bottom hole of jonquil keystone bead, seed bead, teardrop pendant, seed bead, bottom hole of peridot keystone bead, seed bead, teardrop pendant, seed bead, bottom hole of aquamarine keystone bead, seed bead, teardrop pendant, seed bead, bottom hole of crystal AB keystone bead, seed bead, teardrop pendant, seed bead, bottom hole of aquamarine keystone bead, seed bead, teardrop pendant, seed bead, bottom hole of peridot keystone bead, seed bead, teardrop pendant, seed bead, bottom hole of jonquil keystone bead and five seed beads. Pass wire through rondelle already on top wire. Remove bead stopper or tape.

7) Holding both wires together as one, string a crimp tube. Insert wires through other small loop and back through crimp tube, again ensuring chain is on upper portion of loop. Pull slack out of wire. Flatten and fold the crimp tube. Trim excess wire. Set aside extra wire to be used for other two pendants.

8) Repeat steps 1–7 two more times for a total of three pendants.

Earrings

1) Open loop on one ear wire and slip onto center link of 3-inch chain on one pendant. Close loop. Repeat once.

Necklace

1) String one Scrimp finding 1 inch from one end of 20-inch beading wire. Insert short wire tail through a Wire Guardian and 6mm jump ring; insert wire back through Scrimp finding. Secure with screwdriver. Trim short wire tail.

2) String the following: silver round, silver oval, silver round, five liquid silver tubes, silver round, silver oval, silver round and one Pacific opal rondelle. Repeat two more times.

3) String a silver round, silver oval, silver round, two liquid silver tubes, silver round, silver oval, silver round, Pacific opal rondelle, silver round, silver oval and a silver round.

4) Repeat steps 2 and 3 in reverse to string remaining half of necklace.

5) Repeat step 1 to secure wire end to clasp instead of 6mm jump ring.

6) Open 4mm jump ring and slide it onto center link of 3-inch chain on remaining pendant. Attach to center of necklace; close jump ring. ●

Sources: CRYSTALLIZED™ - Swarovski Elements crystals from Fusion Beads; Scrimp findings, Wire Guardians, clasp, crimp tubes and beading wire from Beadalon; chain, sterling silver wire and liquid silver tubes from Fire Mountain Gems and Beads.

easy

black & turquoise

Designs by Helen Rafson

Classic colors and a triple wrap style give this bracelet an everyday wear quality. Try a variation of the earring that suits your taste or make more than one pair. Change the order and number of beads and spacers used in the earrings to create several different looks.

Project note: *Memory wire is hard to cut and will damage regular wire nippers. Always use memory wire shears to cut wire coils.*

INSTRUCTIONS

Earrings

1) String a silver round, silver spacer, light turquoise oval, silver spacer, silver round, nine seed beads and a silver round on a head pin. Form a loop. Trim excess wire with wire nippers. Repeat once.

2) Open loops on ear wires and slide on beaded head pins. Close loops.

Bracelet

1) Form a loop at one end of memory wire. ***Note:*** *Due to the strength of the wire, forming loops of memory wire may take some time.*

2) String seven seed beads, silver round, silver spacer, light turquoise oval, silver spacer, silver round, seven seed beads and a silver round. Repeat 11 more times. String seven seed beads.

3) Form a loop after last bead. Trim excess wire.

Sources: Light turquoise oval beads from Cousin Corp. of America; silver spacers from Hirschberg Schutz & Co. Inc.; memory wire from Beadalon.

MATERIALS

14 (8 x 11mm) light turquoise oval glass beads
42 (3mm) silver round beads
28 silver spacers
193 black seed beads
2 silver head pins
2 silver French ear wires
3½ coils bracelet memory wire
Round-nose pliers
Wire nippers
Memory wire shears or heavy-duty wire cutters

FINISHED SIZES

Earrings
2¼ inches long

Bracelet
Approximately 7½ inches (adjusts to fit most wrists)

intermediate

summer festival

Designs by Melissa Lee

I came back from a recent visit to New York City with a bag full of brightly colored plastic flower beads. I wanted to make something lavish and summery, and this set was the result. I hope you like them as much as I do.

INSTRUCTIONS

Earrings

1) Attach one 5mm jump ring to loop on ear wire. Open a second 5mm jump ring and attach it to top of one koi pendant and to jump ring attached to ear wire. Close ring. Repeat once.

2) String a Czech glass bead and one 13mm (5-petal) flower bead onto a head pin. Form a wrapped loop; trim excess wire. Repeat for each of the following flower beads: one 13mm 5-petal, two 6-petal and two roses.

3) Attach a 6mm jump ring to two ovate-shaped leaf beads and two palmate-shaped leaf beads.

4) Open one 8mm jump ring and string flower and leaf beads, one of each style from steps 2 and 3. Attach jump ring to bottom of one koi pendant; close jump ring.

5) Repeat step 4 for second earring.

Bracelet

Project note: *There is no set pattern to attach the flower and leaf beads to the bracelet. The easiest way to construct the bracelet is to lay out the flower and leaf beads on a bead board and determine arrangement you like best before attaching them to chain.*

1) Use a 5mm jump ring to attach koi button to end link of chain.

2) Slide a pink faceted teardrop onto a 6mm jump ring; attach ring to 5mm jump ring attached to koi button. Close ring.

3) String a Czech glass bead and a flower bead (top down) onto a head pin. Form a wrapped loop, attaching loop to a chain link before wrapping. Trim excess wire.

continued on page 169

MATERIALS

27mm koi button
2 (29 x 26mm) koi pendants
3 (30 x 28mm) pink faceted plastic teardrop beads
Plastic flower beads in shades of pink, violet and red:
- 9 (20mm) roses,
- 10 (28mm) 6-petal,
- 5 (13mm) 5-petal,
- 9 (19mm) 5-petal,
- 6 (28 x 14mm) bell-shaped, 4 (11 x 9mm) tulip-shaped

Green leaf beads:
- 7 (31 x 23mm) palmate-shaped, 9 (19 x 11mm) ovate-shaped,
- 6 (28 x 26mm) heart-shaped

Faceted Czech glass beads:
- 28 (4mm) pink,
- 11 (3mm) clear

Sterling silver jump rings:
- 23 (6mm), 6 (5mm), 2 (8mm)

43 (2-inch) sterling silver head pins
2 sterling silver screwback-style earring findings
Sterling silver lobster-claw clasp
8 inches 6 x 4mm sterling silver oval-link chain
Round-nose pliers
Chain-nose pliers
Wire nippers

FINISHED SIZES

Earrings
3 inches long

Bracelet
8¾ inches (including clasp)

easy

black onyx set

Designs by Sandy Parpart

Black and silver go with everything in your wardrobe, giving this set a timeless quality. Perfect with a little black dress or jeans and a sweater.

Project note: *String bead caps so they "cup" the black diamond crystals.*

INSTRUCTIONS

Earrings

1) String the following onto a head pin: sterling silver round, bead cap, black diamond bicone, bead cap and a sterling silver round bead. Form a wrapped loop. Trim excess wire. Repeat once.

2) Open loops on ear wires and slide on beaded head pins; close loops.

Bracelet

1) String a crimp bead ½ inch from one end of beading wire; insert short wire tail through clasp and back through crimp bead. Use crimp pliers to flatten and fold the crimp bead.

2) String a bead cap, black diamond bicone, bead cap, two black onyx beads, bead cap, black diamond bicone, bead cap and a black onyx bead. Repeat three more times. The last sequence will not have the single black onyx bead.

3) String a crimp bead. Insert wire through jump ring and back through crimp bead and several other beads. Flatten and fold the crimp bead. Trim excess wire.

Sources: Black onyx beads and CRYSTALLIZED™ - Swarovski Elements from Fusion Beads; crimp beads and beading wire from Beadalon.

MATERIALS

11 (8mm) black onyx round beads
10 (8mm) black diamond CRYSTALLIZED™ - Swarovski Elements bicone crystals
4 (3mm) sterling silver round beads
20 (6 x 3mm) sterling silver bead caps
5mm sterling silver jump ring
2 (1½-inch) 24-gauge sterling silver head pins
2 (1.3mm) silver crimp beads
2 sterling silver fishhook ear wires
6 x 10mm sterling silver lobster-claw clasp
9½ inches .018-inch-diameter 7-strand nylon-coated flexible beading wire
Round-nose pliers
Chain-nose pliers
Crimp pliers
Flush cutters

FINISHED SIZES

Earrings
1½ inches long

Bracelet
7¾ inches (including clasp)

easy

anastasia

Designs by Molly Schaller

Anastasia goes to the opera and wears her favorite jewels to reflect the soft theater lights. Understated but gorgeous, this piece uses flat-back crystals and natural brass filigree for a combination with nostalgic romance.

INSTRUCTIONS

1) Use bead cement to glue one 3mm flat-back crystal to center of each deco bar connector. Embellish filigree pendant as shown, using 4mm flat-back crystal in the center. Set aside and let dry overnight.

2) Slide a bead cap, Pacific opal crystal and a bead cap onto a head pin, stringing caps so they "cup" the crystal. Form a loop. Trim excess wire. Repeat once.

3) Repeat step 2 with indicolite crystals for a total of four beaded dangles, two indicolite and two Pacific opal.

4) Slide a bead cap, crystal and a bead cap onto an eye pin. Form a loop; trim excess wire. Repeat for each remaining crystal for a total of 15 links, seven indicolite links and eight Pacific opal links.

5) To assemble earrings, attach one Pacific opal dangle to a connector. Open loop on an ear wire and pass it through opposite end of connector. Close loop. Repeat for second earring.

6) To assemble necklace, open links to attach components as follows: clasp hook, 7.25mm jump ring, 4mm jump ring, connector, Pacific opal link, connector, indicolite link, connector, Pacific opal link, connector, indicolite link, 7.25mm jump ring, indicolite link, connector, Pacific opal link, 7.25mm jump ring, Pacific opal link, connector, indicolite link, 7.25mm jump ring, indicolite link, connector, Pacific opal link, connector, indicolite link, connector, Pacific opal link, connector, 4mm jump ring, 7.25mm jump ring and clasp loop.

7) Open loops and connect the following: indicolite dangle, connector and Pacific opal link. Repeat once. Attach assembled dangles to 7.25mm jump rings on either side of center of necklace.

8) For center pendant dangle, open loop on an indicolite link and connect to top of filigree pendant. Attach dangle to center 7.25mm jump ring.

Sources: Brass components from Vintaj Natural Brass Co.; crystals from CRYSTALLIZED™ - Swarovski Elements.

MATERIALS

8mm CRYSTALLIZED™ - Swarovski Elements rondelles: 10 Pacific opal, 9 indicolite

Indicolite CRYSTALLIZED™ - Swarovski Elements flat-back crystals: 19 (3mm), 1 (4mm)

14 (3 x 18mm) 2-hole deco bar connectors

26 x 55mm Etruscan drop filigree pendant

38 (8mm) Etruscan bead caps

15 (1-inch) brass eye pins

4 (1-inch) brass head pins

Brass jump rings: 2 (4mm), 5 (7.25mm)

2 brass ear wires

35 x 11mm brass hook-and-eye clasp set

Round-nose pliers

Chain-nose pliers

Flush cutters

Bead cement

FINISHED SIZES

Earrings

1½ inches long

Necklace

15⅜ inches (including clasp)

intermediate

love code set

Designs by Melissa Lee

I am really a bit of a geek at heart. I love the way binary code looks, and I thought it would make a great design element in a piece of jewelry. The fine silver pendant spells out "love" in binary code, with a heart in place of one of the zeroes. The earring charms also contain part of the code for "love," again with hearts in place of two of the zeroes.

INSTRUCTIONS

Earrings

1) Form a wrapped loop at one end of one 3-inch piece of 24-gauge wire attaching loop to top of a Geek Love charm before wrapping.

2) String one black onyx rondelle, one peridot rondelle and one black onyx rondelle. Form another wrapped loop, attaching loop to ear wire before wrapping. Trim excess wire.

3) String one black onyx teardrop onto center of a 3-inch piece of 24-gauge wire. Bend both wire ends up above top of teardrop; wrap one wire around the other just above bead, securing bead in place. Form a wrapped loop with other wire end, attaching loop to bottom of Geek Love charm before wrapping. Trim excess wire.

4) Repeat steps 1–3 for second earring.

Necklace

Project note: *When working with epoxy, always work in a well-ventilated area and follow manufacturer's safety instructions.*

1) String a crimp bead ½ inch from one end of beading wire; insert short wire tail through one jump ring and back through crimp bead. Use crimp pliers to flatten the crimp bead.

MATERIALS

Geek Love fine silver pendant
2 Geek Love fine silver round charms
Faceted rondelles:
 26 (9 x 4mm) peridot,
 16 (4 x 2.5mm) black onyx
2 (28 x 10mm) black onyx faceted teardrop beads
4 (6mm) 16-gauge sterling silver jump rings
2 (1.3mm) sterling silver crimp beads
2 (9mm) fine silver end caps
2 sterling silver ear wires
2 sterling silver lobster-claw clasps
4 (3-inch) pieces 24-gauge sterling silver wire
6 (8½-inch) pieces 1.5mm black leather cord
10 inches .012-inch-diameter nylon-coated flexible beading wire
Round-nose pliers
Chain-nose pliers
Crimp pliers
Wire nippers
Rubber gloves
Alcohol pad
Toothpicks
Epoxy

FINISHED SIZES

Earrings

3½ inches long

Necklace

17¼ inches (including clasp)

2) String 12 peridot rondelles.

3) Insert wire through one side of pendant. String 12 black onyx rondelles. Insert wire through other side of pendant.

4) Repeat step 2.

5) String a crimp bead; insert wire through a jump ring and back through crimp bead and two or three rondelles. Flatten the crimp bead. Trim excess wire. Set beaded wire aside.

6) Wipe down ends of leather cords and insides of end caps with alcohol pad. Allow end caps and cords to dry thoroughly. ***Note:*** *Do not touch them with your bare hands afterwards, as the oil from your hands will leave a residue and may prevent the epoxy from adhering properly.*

7) Wear rubber gloves and mix a small batch of epoxy according to manufacturer's instructions. Apply a layer of epoxy to interiors of end caps and to ends of leather cords using a toothpick.

8) Insert leather cords into end caps. Allow epoxy to dry according to manufacturer's instructions.

9) Use jump rings to attach a clasp to each end cap.

10) To complete necklace, attach clasps to jump rings at ends of beaded wire.

Sources: Geek Love pendant, charms and end caps from Melissa J. Lee; black onyx rondelles and epoxy from Chelsea's Beads; black onyx teardrop beads from String A Strand; peridot rondelles, clasps, jump rings, crimp beads, ear wires, 24-gauge wire and beading wire from Fire Mountain Gems and Beads; leather cord from Riverstone Bead Co.

ombre leaves

continued from page 132

8) Form a loop at one end of trimmed wire from step 7. String a fuchsia bicone. Form a loop; trim excess wire. Open loop and attach to top of leaf connector.

9) Open top loop of beaded wire and attach to ear wire; close loop.

10) Repeat steps 7–9 for second earring.

11) For a variation on this earring, create this design with a single color of clay, condition clay and roll it out on thickest setting and start from step 6. ***Note:*** *The olive green is created by using three parts gold to one part turquoise. Mix colors together thoroughly.*

Source: All materials from Michaels Stores Inc.

sand & sky

continued from page 152

9) Open another 8mm jump ring; slide it through wrapped loop of beaded eye pin from step 1 and brass hammered ring. Close jump ring.

Sources: African yellow stone saucers from Dakota Stones; turquoise rondelle and black onyx beads from Fire Mountain Gems and Beads; lava rock from Harlequin Beads & Jewelry; yellow jasper beads from Lima Beads; Earthy aqua lampwork glass beads (inspired by the glass art of Gartner & Blade Glass) from Isinglass Design; CRYSTALLIZED™ - Swarovski Elements crystal pearls from Artbeads.com; 8mm and 10mm brass rings and S clasp from Rishashay.

a little twisted

continued from page 140

5) Open jump rings at ends and attach clasp ends; close rings.

6) String a pillow bead on a head pin; form a wrapped loop. Trim excess wire. Repeat for each remaining pillow bead. ***Note:*** *Before forming wrapped spiral loop on one of the rectangle beads, attach loop to round end of clasp.*

7) Open center jump ring between each link and slide on remaining beaded head pins; close rings.

Source: Thai pillow beads from Twinklehut.

summer festival

continued from page 160

4) Repeat step 3 for each remaining flower bead. ***Note:*** *For tulip-shaped beads, omit the Czech glass bead.*

5) Use 6mm jump rings to attach leaf beads to chain interspersed between flower beads.

6) To finish, use a 5mm jump ring to attach lobster-claw clasp to final link.

Sources: Koi pendants and button from Melissa J. Lee; flower and leaf beads and teardrop beads from Toho Shoji N.Y.; Czech glass beads from Kasie's Beads; chain from Ayla's Originals; screwback-style earring findings from Turtle Island Beads; lobster-claw clasp from Fire Mountain Gems and Beads.

metric conversion charts

METRIC CONVERSIONS				
yards	x	.9144	=	metres (m)
yards	x	91.44	=	centimetres (cm)
inches	x	2.54	=	centimetres (cm)
inches	x	25.40	=	millimetres (mm)
inches	x	.0254	=	metres (m)

centimetres	x	.3937	=	inches
metres	x	1.0936	=	yards

INCHES INTO MILLIMETRES & CENTIMETRES (Rounded off slightly)

inches	mm	cm	inches	cm	inches	cm	inches	cm
1/8	3	0.3	5	12.5	21	53.5	38	96.5
1/4	6	0.6	5 1/2	14	22	56	39	99
3/8	10	1	6	15	23	58.5	40	101.5
1/2	13	1.3	7	18	24	61	41	104
5/8	15	1.5	8	20.5	25	63.5	42	106.5
3/4	20	2	9	23	26	66	43	109
7/8	22	2.2	10	25.5	27	68.5	44	112
1	25	2.5	11	28	28	71	45	114.5
1 1/4	32	3.2	12	30.5	29	73.5	46	117
1 1/2	38	3.8	13	33	30	76	47	119.5
1 3/4	45	4.5	14	35.5	31	79	48	122
2	50	5	15	38	32	81.5	49	124.5
2 1/2	65	6.5	16	40.5	33	84	50	127
3	75	7.5	17	43	34	86.5		
3 1/2	90	9	18	46	35	89		
4	100	10	19	48.5	36	91.5		
4 1/2	115	11.5	20	51	37	94		

photo index

photo index

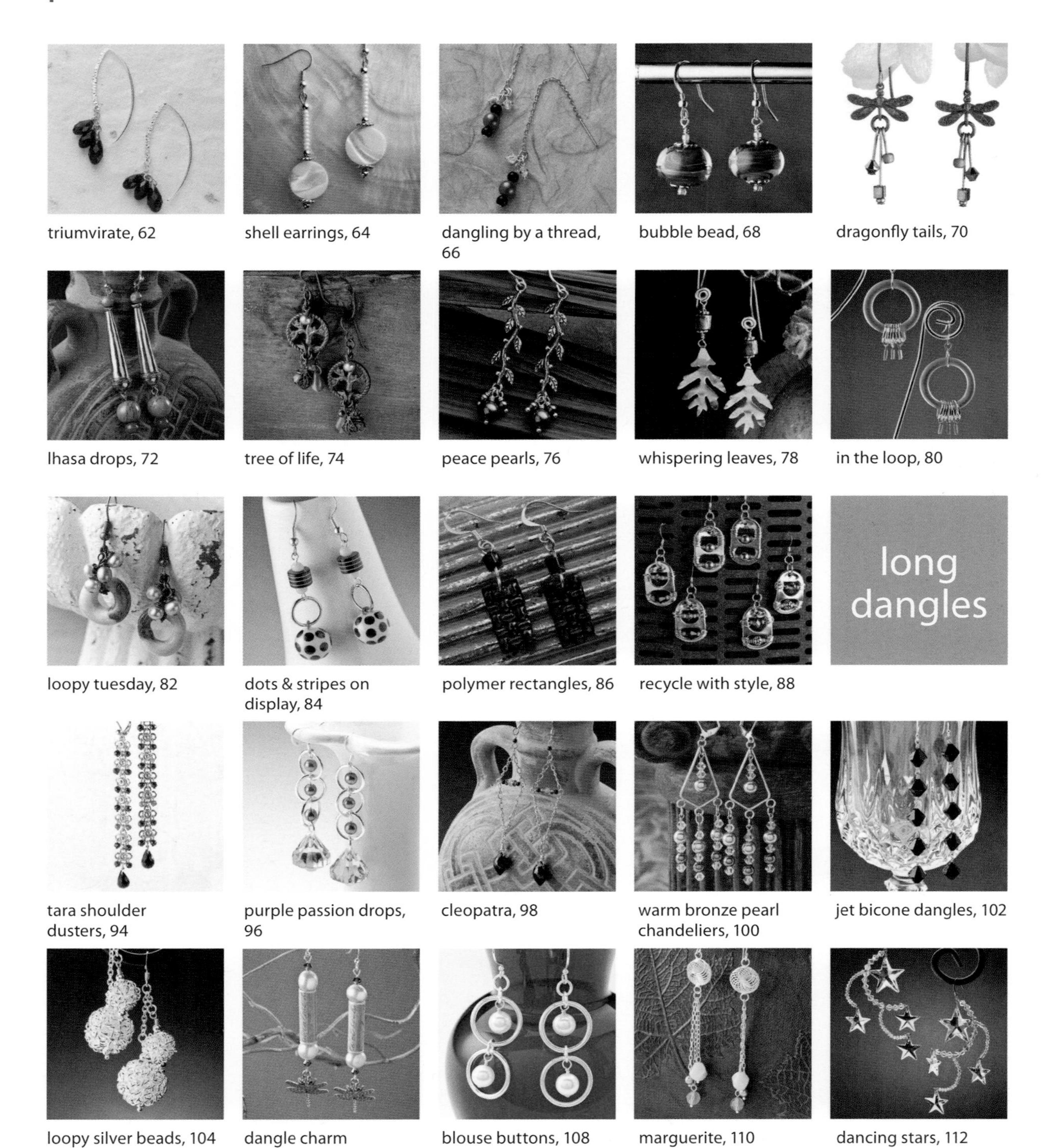

photo index

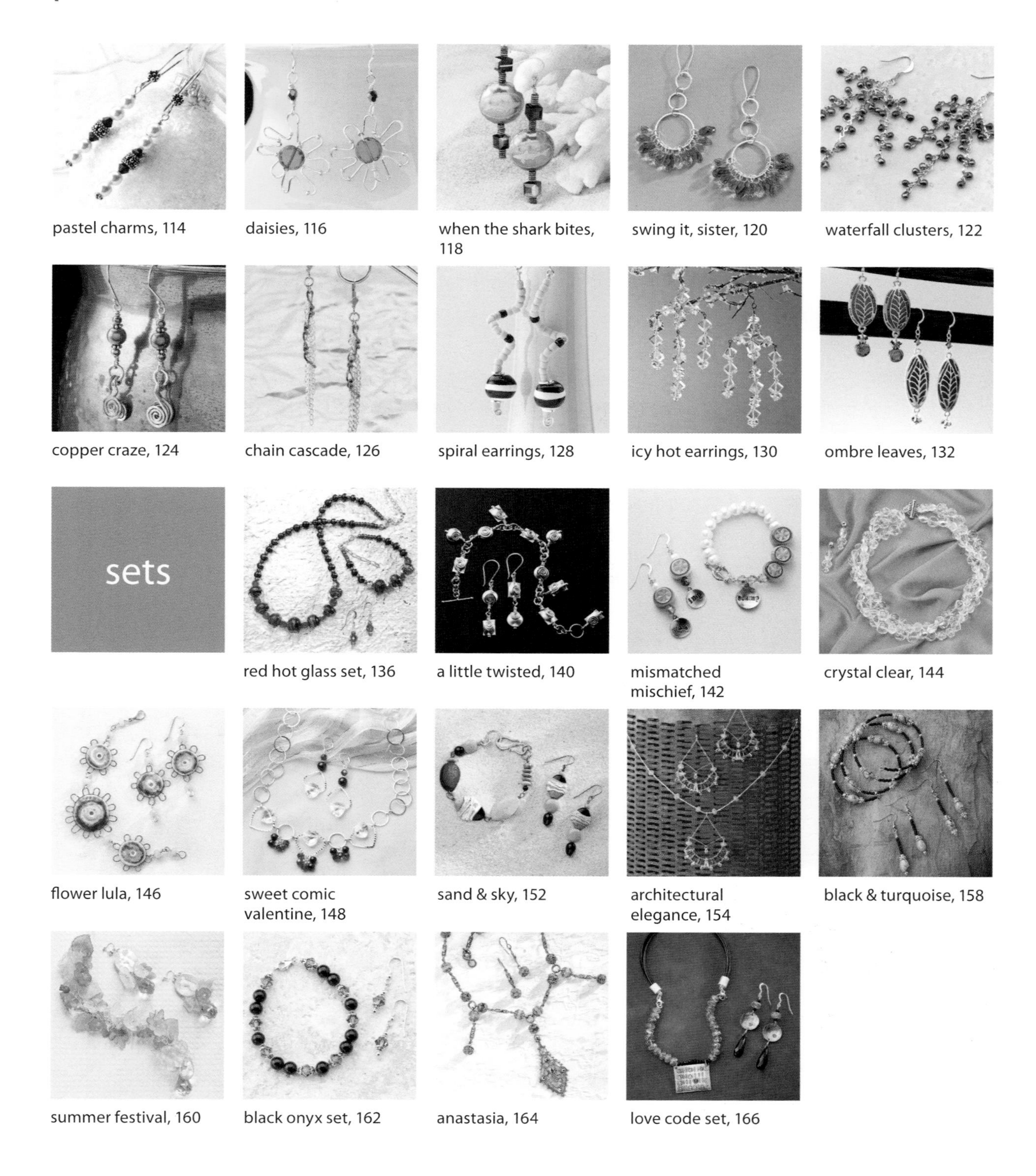

buyer's guide

Due to the ever-changing nature of the bead industry, it may be impossible to find the exact beads and components used in the designs shown in this publication. Similar beads may be found via the Internet or by visiting your local bead shops and shows. Making substitutions is encouraged by the editor, as it adds a personal touch.

A.C. Moore Inc.
(888) ACMOORE (226-6673)
(Option 2)
www.acmoore.com

Artbeads.com
(866) 715-BEAD (2323)
www.artbeads.com

ARTchix Studio
(250) 478-5985
www.artchixstudio.com

Ayla's Originals
(877) 328-AYLA (2952)
www.aylasoriginals.com

Bead Trust
(510) 540-5815
www.beadtrust.com

Beadalon
(866) 4BEADALON (423-2325)
www.beadalon.com

p. 76

Beaded Impressions Inc.
(800) 532-8480
www.abeadstore.com

Bijoux Collection
(818) 344-3110

Blue Moon Beads
(800) 727-2727
www.creativityinc.com

Brightlings Beads
(919) 388-9822
www.brightlingsbeads.com

Capilano Rock & Gem
(604) 987-5311
www.capilanorock.ca

Caravan Beads Inc.
(800) 230-8941
www.caravanbeads.com

Charlene's Beads
(760) 948-6184
www.cbbeads.com

Chelsea's Beads
(847) 433-3451
www.chelseasbeads.com

Cindy Gimbrone Beads
www.cindygimbronebeads.com

Clearsnap Inc.
(888) 448-4862
www.clearsnap.com

Clearwater Beads
(888) 91BEADS (912-3237)
www.clearwaterbeads.com

Cousin Corp. of America
(727) 536-3568
www.cousin.com

Creative Impressions in Clay
(513) 755-2155
www.claybuttons.com

CRYSTALLIZED™ - Swarovski Elements
www.crystallized.com

Dakota Stones
(866) 871-1990
www.dakotastones.com

Darice Inc.
(866) 4Darice (432-7423)
www.darice.com

E. A. Revit Inc.
(570) 287-1376

Earthstone Co.
www.earthstone.com

Fernando Dasilva Jewelry
(214) 766-8354
www.dasilvajewelry.com

Fire Mountain Gems and Beads
(800) 355-2137
www.firemountaingems.com

Frabels Inc.
(514) 842-8561
www.frabels.com

Fusion Beads
www.fusionbeads.com

Galena Beads
(815) 777-4080
www.galenabeads.com

Glass Bead Store
www.glassbeadstore.com

Glass Garden Beads
www.glassgardenbeads.com

Halcraft USA
(914) 840-0505
www.halcraft.com

Harlequin Beads & Jewelry
(888) 683-5903
www.harlequinbeads.com

Hirschberg Schutz & Co. Inc.
(908) 810-1111

Hobby Lobby Stores Inc.
www.hobbylobby.com

Humblebeads
(210) 785-8981
www.humblebeads.com

Isinglass Design
www.glassbead.etsy.com

Jangles
(706) 207-9032
www.jangles.net

Jayamahe Bali
www.bali-beads.com

Jo-Ann Stores Inc.
www.joann.com

Kasie's Beads
(630) 357-8931
www.kasiesbeads.com

Kazuri West
www.kazuriwest.com

Lima Beads
(888) 211-7919
www.limabeads.com

Makin's Clay
www.makinsclay.com

Martha Stewart Crafts
www.marthastewartcrafts.com

**Marvin Schwab/
The Bead Warehouse**
(301) 565-0487
www.thebeadwarehouse.com

Melissa J. Lee
www.melissajlee.etsy.com

Michaels Stores Inc.
(800) MICHAELS (642-4235)
www.michaels.com

Mode Beads
(718) 765-0124
www.modebeads.com

Nina Designs
(800) 336-6462
www.ninadesigns.com

Objects and Elements
(206) 965-0373
www.objectsandelements.com

Oriental Trading Co.
(800) 875-8480
www.orientaltrading.com

Plaid Enterprises Inc.
(800) 842-4197
www.plaidonline.com

Rings & Things
(800) 366-2156
www.rings-things.com

Rishashay
(800) 517-3311
www.rishashay.com

Riverstone Bead Co.
(219) 939-2050
www.riverstonebead.com

RupaB Designs
(510) 791-6135
www.rupab.com

Sarah Moran
www.z-beads.com

Sassy Silkies/Kristal Wick
(866) 811-1376
www.sassysilkies.com

Shiana
www.shiana.com

Somerset Silver Inc.
(425) 641-3666
www.somerset-silver.com

String A Strand
(888) 858-4414
www.string-a-strand.com

Thunderbird Supply Co.
(800) 545-7968
www.thunderbirdsupply.com

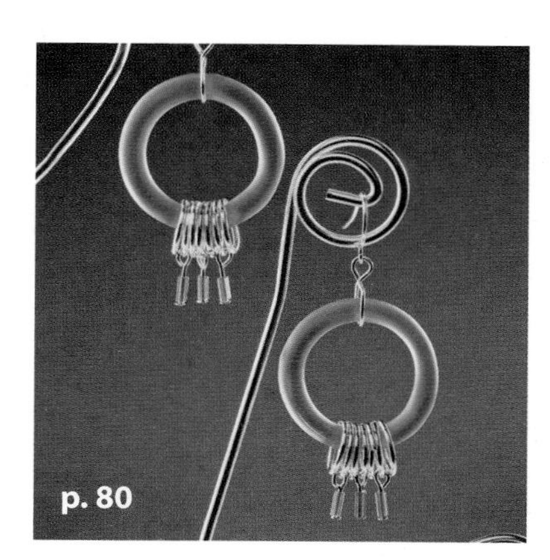
p. 80

Toho Shoji N.Y.
(212) 868-7465
www.tohoshoji-ny.com

Tsukineko Inc.
(800) 769-6633
www.tsukineko.com

Tucson Mountain Jewelry
www.tucsonmountainjewels.com

Turtle Island Beads
(608) 356-8823
www.turtleislandbeads.com

Twinklehut
(662) 564-0668
www.twinklehut.com

Unit Tool Co.
(401) 781-2647
www.unittoolco.com

Via Murano
(877) 842-6872
www.viamurano.com

Vintaj Natural Brass Co.
www.vintaj.com

Wal-Mart Stores Inc.
www.wal-mart.com

Wonder Sources Inc.
(888) 999-0478
www.wondersources.com

The Buyer's Guide listings are provided as a service to our readers and should not be considered an endorsement from this publication.

special thanks

Caito Amorose
dancing stars, 112
icy hot earrings, 130

Rupa Balachandar
hoopla, 22
hyacinth honey, 54
lhasa drops, 72

Candie Cooper
fabric love, 40

Laurie D'Ambrosio
dangling by a thread, 66
in the loop, 80
polymer rectangles, 86

E.A. Revit Inc.
egyptian earrings, 48
recycle with style, 88
daisies, 116

Fernando DaSilva Jewelry
wrapped hoops, 18
tara shoulder dusters, 94
sweet comic valentine, 148

Fusion Beads
night fall, 14
juxt, 56
blouse buttons, 108
chain cascade, 126

Ishita Ghosh
sand & sky, 152

Brenda Morris Jarrett
whispering leaves, 78

Camilla Jorgenson
urban jungle, 28
starbursts, 32
beach fun, 36

Jangles
spiral earrings, 128
flower lula, 146

Melissa Lee
mismatched mischief, 142
summer festival, 160
love code set, 166

Laura McIvor
copper craze, 124
a little twisted, 140

Sandy Parpart
warm bronze pearl chandeliers, 100
jet bicone dangles, 102
black onyx set, 162

Margot Potter
oceans of delight, 20
crystal stash, 44
swing it, sister, 120

Heather Powers
garden lantern hoops, 16
ombre leaves, 132

Helen Rafson
shell earrings, 64
black & turquoise, 158

Carole Rodgers
loopy silver beads, 104
waterfall clusters, 122

Sassy Silkies
sassy silkies posts, 26
relique earrings, 52
dangle charm earrings, 106

Molly Schaller
cindi, 50
kaia's dream, 60
cleopatra, 98
marguerite, 110
architectural elegance, 154
anastasia, 164

Barb Switzer
triumvirate, 62
peace pearls, 76
loopy tuesday, 82

Tucson Mountain Jewelry
rustic essence, 30
royal elegance, 34
sweet medley, 58
pastel charms, 114

VINTAJ Natural Brass Co.
beautiful flight, 42
dragonfly tails, 70
tree of life, 74

The Glass Bead Store
bubble bead, 68
red hot glass set, 136

Alexa Westerfield
sassy sequin hoops, 24
feelin' the blues, 46
dots & stripes on display, 84
purple passion drops, 96

Suzann Wilson
crystal clear, 144

Jean Yates
when the shark bites, 118

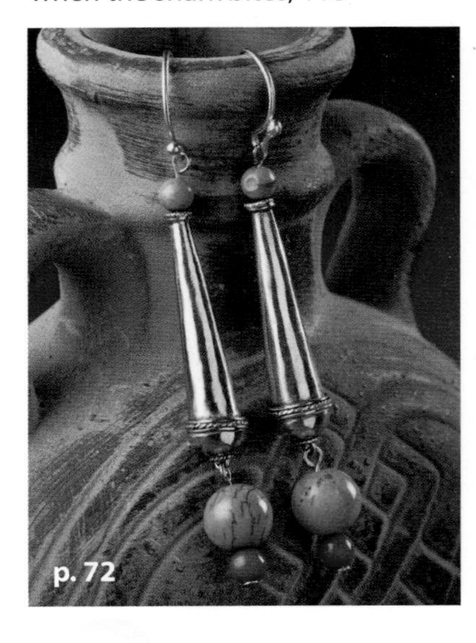
p. 72